FUN MATHEMATICS
ON YOUR MICROCOMPUTER

CZES KOSNIOWSKI

University of Newcastle upon Tyne

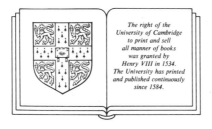

The right of the
University of Cambridge
to print and sell
all manner of books
was granted by
Henry VIII in 1534.
The University has printed
and published continuously
since 1584.

CAMBRIDGE UNIVERSITY PRESS
Cambridge
London New York New Rochelle
Melbourne Sydney

Published by the Press Syndicate of the University of Cambridge
The Pitt Building, Trumpington Street, Cambridge CB2 1RP
32 East 57th Street, New York, NY 10022, USA
296 Beaconsfield Parade, Middle Park, Melbourne 3206, Australia

© Cambridge University Press 1983

First published 1983
Reprinted 1983, 1984

Typeset by the author using an ACT Sirius 1 microcomputer, together with an ACT Wordstar word processor and an ACT Daisywheel printer.

Printed in Great Britain at the University Press, Cambridge

Library of Congress catalogue card number: 83-1811

British Library cataloguing in publication data
Kosniowski, C.
Fun mathematics for your microcomputer
1. Mathematics—Data processing
2. Microprocessors
I. Title
510'.28'5404   QA76.95

ISBN 0 521 27451 6

CONTENTS

START HERE, an introduction   1

AND SO ON...FOREVER, about sequences and series   7

UP AND DOWN, ROUND AND ROUND, about functions, graphs and polar coordinates   29

5 MILES NORTH, 4 MILES EAST, about geometry   51

STRETCHING AND SHRINKING, about matrices   57

PLAYING THE GAME, about games of strategy   65

REARRANGING THINGS, about groups   87

WAIT, about the theory of queues or lines   107

PRETTY PICTURES, about functions of two variables   129

ON THE MOVE, about differential equations   145

GETTING BIGGER ALL THE TIME, more on differential equations   167

APPENDIX – CONVERTING YOUR PROGRAM, notes to help you convert the programs   185

WHERE IT IS, an index   193

THANKS

The author is indebted to ACT (Pulsar) Ltd and ACT (Sirius) Ltd for their help and advice. It is a pleasure indeed to find a company that not only supplies an excellent product but also provides an excellent back-up service. Indeed, seeing is believing.

Thanks are also due to the many manufacturers that willingly supplied photographs of their computers.

The author also wishes to thank the Computing Department of the University of Newcastle upon Tyne for use of their computer, and for permission to use some graphs and diagrams produced with the computer.

Finally, many thanks to Ann, Kora and Inga for their unfailing support and for being guinea-pigs for many of the programs in this book.

START HERE
an introduction

The theme of this book is that you can have fun while exploring the fascinating world of mathematics on your microcomputer. Each chapter introduces some important part of mathematics. The basic ideas are explained and are then incorporated into computer programs. These programs are usually in the form of an entertaining game. Sometimes the program provides vivid and beautiful pictures.

If you have wondered how you can use your computer to learn something useful while having fun, then this is the book for you. You do not have to be an expert in either mathematics or computing to enjoy this book. Whether you have a low cost home computer, a sophisticated home computer, an educational computer, or a business system computer you will find this book useful.

All the programs have been written in BASIC and have been written in such a way that they are readily adaptable to your own computer. Some conversion notes are given in the Appendix.

The program listings have been printed directly from bug-free running programs. The programs have been tested on several different home computers. Throughout the book, sample screen printouts are provided. These show you what you should see on your screen when the program is running.

The chapters are relatively independent of one another. There is therefore no need to start with the first chapter.

This book will teach you something about computing and mathematics. It will provide you with an endless source of ideas. What you learn will enable you to write your own even more sophisticated programs.

A very brief outline of each chapter follows.

And so on ... forever. Sequences and series crop up all over the place. You will find them with caterpillars crawling on elastic, while making snowflakes and with confused but loving husbands. A game based on intelligence tests will keep you busy for hours.

Up and down, round and round. This chapter explores graph plotting and includes a program enabling you to "zoom" in on any interesting parts of a graph. You will find out about "polar honey bees" and how to create an endless number of pretty pictures.

5 miles North, 4 miles East. This contains a brief account about geometry and distance. A game called TREASURE HUNT is included.

Stretching and shrinking. Here you will discover how to stretch and shrink any pictures you have on your screen. It is all done with matrices.

Playing the game. There is a topic in mathematics called game theory. It is about games of strategy and provides a good source of games for home computers. You can play with an investment game, learn about a beer drinking game and possibly make money with one of the games.

Rearranging things. The word groups is now familiar to many because of Rubik's cube. This chapter contains some of the basic ideas in group theory such as permutations, transpositions and cycles. Included are several computer games based on group theory. These are entertaining as well as being educational.

Wait. We have all stood waiting in a line or queue. Here you will learn some of the main ideas behind the theory of queues and you will have fun playing games based on queues.

Pretty pictures. This chapter is about three-dimensional pictures and contour maps. You will be able to produce many beautiful pictures and patterns.

On the move.   Getting bigger all the time. What do bouncing balls, aeroplanes and bacteria have in common? The answer is differential equations. These two chapters look into differential equations. Have fun simulating the flying of aeroplanes and rockets. Also, try to save a room full of people dying from a deadly virus.

Appendix – converting your program. Each program in this book has been written so that it is readily adaptable to your home computer. This chapter will help you make any necessary alterations to the programs.

Note. Because the programs are readily adaptable to any microcomputer they are consequently not as "neat" or "short" as they could be if they had been written for one specific machine. You can shorten, and possibly improve, many of the programs in this book. Part of the fun of computing is rewriting programs and adding your own personal touch.

A word about computer models. Some of the programs in this book are based, loosely, on the real world. They model the real world. It is very important not to confuse any of these models with reality itself. Obviously a model is useful if it resembles reality closely. But models will always predict things that will not occur. And things that in reality occur may not be predicted by the model. Models are useful because they help explain why certain things happen. They provide suggestions for what may happen. Computer models provide answers very quickly. Do not be misled by computer models.

Some popular microcomputers. Home computer systems vary in price and sophistication. The next three pages contain photographs of some of the popular microcomputers. They have been divided, in an approximate way, into three categories depending upon price and sophistication. It was impossible to include photographs of every microcomputer. The photographs are representative but by no means exhaustive. Do not worry if your computer does not appear in the photographs - you will still find this book both useful and rewarding.

START HERE

START HERE

AND SO ON...FOREVER

about sequences and series

Suppose you are given £10 this week with a promise that each week you will receive an increase of £2. How much will you receive in the fifteenth week? What is the total amount received during these fifteen weeks?

It is not too difficult to write down a list (or **sequence**) of numbers indicating the amount received each week.

10, 12, 14, 16, 18, 20, 22, 24, 26, 28, 30, 32, 34, 36, 38

Such a list is called an arithmetic sequence or arithmetic progression; the numbers in the sequence are called the **terms** of the sequence. You should have no difficulty in writing down further terms in this sequence.

In general an **arithmetic sequence** is a sequence in which the difference between each term and the next one is constant. We may write down an arithmetic sequence, using symbols, in the following way.

A, A+D, A+2*D, A+3*D, ..., A+(N-1)*D

Here A is the first term in the sequence, D is the common difference and N is the number of terms in the sequence. The "..." is used to save us writing down every term, you may think of it as "and so on until". Some further examples of arithmetic sequences are given below.

5, 2, -1, -4, -7	(A = 5, D = -3, N = 5)
0, 0.5, 1, 1.5, 2, 2.5, 3	(A = 0, D = 0.5, N = 7)
1, 1.3, 1.6, 1.9, 2.2, 2.5	(A = 1, D = 0.3, N = 6)
1, 3, 5, 7, 9, ..., 99	(A = 1, D = 2, N = 50)

Frequently, we want to find the sum of a number of terms in a sequence. For example,

   5 + 2 + -1 + -4 + -7, and
   1 + 3 + 5 + 7 + 9 + ... + 99

We call these expressions **arithmetic series**. There is a formula for arithmetic series; this will be given shortly. You may recognise the next formula.

   1 + 2 + 3 + 4 + ... + N = N*(N+1)/2

Thus, for example, the sum of the first ten numbers is 55. The general formula for other arithmetic series is given below.

   A + (A+D) + (A+2*D) + ... + (A+(N-1)*D) = A*N + D*(N-1)*N/2

Returning to our original problem we see that the amount received during the fifteen weeks is 10*15 + 2*14*15/2, which is £360.

You can create arithmetic sequences quite easily with the program ARITHMETIC SEQUENCES. You INPUT the first term, the common difference and the number of terms you require. The sequence will be printed out, together with the sum of all the terms in the sequence. Notice that in this program each term in the sequence is calculated by adding the common difference D to the previous term.

The numbering in ARITHMETIC SEQUENCES and the next three programs has been arranged so that the four programs may be incorporated into a single program entitled SEQUENCES AND SERIES. Each of the four programs are independent of one another and will RUN without the other ones.

```
1010 REM               *************************
1020 REM               *                       *
1030 REM               * ARITHMETIC SEQUENCES  *
1040 REM               *                       *
1050 REM               *************************
1060 REM
1070 REM
1100 REM ///////////////////// INPUT DATA /////////////////////////////
1110 PRINT CHR$(147) : REM CLEAR SCREEN
1120 PRINT "ARITHMETIC SEQUENCES"
1130 PRINT
1140 PRINT "FIRST TERM ";
1150 INPUT A
1160 PRINT
```

See the Appendix for some general program notes.

```
1170 PRINT "COMMON DIFFERENCE ";
1180 INPUT D
1190 PRINT
1200 PRINT "NUMBER OF TERMS ";
1210 INPUT N
1300 REM %%%%%%%%%%%%%%%%%%%%%% CALCULATE AND DISPLAY %%%%%%%%%%%%%%%%%%%%%%
1310 PRINT
1320 PRINT "THE SEQUENCE:"
1330 PRINT
1340 LET TERM=A
1350 LET SUM=0
1360 FOR I=1 TO N
1370 PRINT TERM;
1380 LET SUM=SUM+TERM
1390 LET TERM=TERM+D
1400 NEXT I
1410 PRINT
1420 PRINT
1430 PRINT "SUM IS ";SUM
1440 PRINT
1500 REM %%%%%%%%%%%%%%%%%%%%%% ENDING AND ANOTHER GO %%%%%%%%%%%%%%%%%%%%%%
1510 PRINT " ANOTHER GO? Y OR N"
1520 GET G$ : REM LET G$=INKEY$
1530 IF G$<>"Y" AND G$<>"N" THEN GOTO 1520
1540 IF G$="Y" THEN GOTO 1110
```

```
ARITHMETIC SEQUENCES

FIRST TERM ? -7

COMMON DIFFERENCE ? 3

NUMBER OF TERMS ? 5

THE SEQUENCE:

-7  -4  -1   2   5

SUM IS -5

  ANOTHER GO?   Y OR N
```

Another common type of sequence is the geometric sequence or geometric progression. This is illustrated by an example. Suppose, once again, that you are given £10 this week but now with a 10% increase each week. How much will you receive in the fifteenth week? What is the total amount received during these fifteen weeks?

Part of the sequence of numbers representing the amount received each week is given below. Each number should be rounded to two decimal places if we want the answer in £s.

10, 11, 12.1, 13.31, 14.641, 16.1051, 17.71561, ...

The amount on the fifteenth week will be £37.97.

A **geometric sequence** is a sequence in which the ratio between one term and the next one is constant. In the example above each term is obtained from the previous term by multiplying it by 1.1. Using symbols we can write down a geometric sequence in the following way.

$A, A*R, A*R^2, A*R^3, ..., A*R^{N-1}$

Here A stands for the first term in the sequence, R stands for the common ratio and N stands for the number of terms in the sequence. Also, as usual, R^2 (read as "R squared") means $R*R$ and R^3 (read as "R cubed") means $R*R*R$, etc.

Some further examples of geometric sequences are given below.

    1, 2, 4, 8, 16, 32, 64   (A = 1, R = 2, N = 7)
    4, 2, 1, 0.5, 0.25, 0.125, 0.0625   (A = 4, R = 0.5, N = 7)
    1, -2, 4, -8, 16, -32, 64, -128   (A = 1, R = -2, N = 8)

The sum of the terms of a geometric sequence is called a **geometric series**. The formula for a geometric series is given below.

$A + A*R + A*R^2 + ... + A*R^{N-1} = A*(1 - R^N)/(1 - R)$

Thus the amount received after fifteen weeks (starting with £10 and receiving a 10% increase each week) is $10*(1 - 1.1^{15})/(1 - 1.1)$, which is approximately £317.72.

The formula given above for the geometric series is not very difficult to derive. Call the sum SUM; thus:

$SUM = A + A*R + A*R^2 + A*R^3 + ... + A*R^{N-1}$

AND SO ON ... FOREVER

If we multiply this equation by R then we obtain a second equation.

$$R*SUM = A*R + A*R^2 + A*R^3 + \ldots + A*R^N$$

Subtracting the second equation from the first gives the following one.

$$SUM - R*SUM = A - A*R^N \quad \text{or} \quad (1 - R)*SUM = A*(1 - R^N)$$

Thus we deduce that SUM = $A*(1 - R^N)/(1 - R)$, as long as R is not equal to 1 (we cannot divide by 0).

You can produce many geometric sequences with the program GEOMETRIC SEQUENCES. You INPUT the first term, the common ratio and the number of terms required. The sequence is then displayed together with the sum of the terms in the sequence.

GEOMETRIC SEQUENCES is an independent program which also forms the second part of the program SEQUENCES AND SERIES.

```
2010 REM               ************************
2020 REM               *                        *
2030 REM               *   GEOMETRIC SEQUENCES  *
2040 REM               *                        *
2050 REM               ************************
2060 REM
2070 REM
2100 REM %%%%%%%%%%%%%%%%%%%%% INPUT DATA %%%%%%%%%%%%%%%%%%%%%%%%%%%%%
2110 PRINT CHR$(147) : REM CLEAR SCREEN
2120 PRINT "GEOMETRIC SEQUENCES"
2130 PRINT
2140 PRINT "FIRST TERM ";
2150 INPUT A
2160 PRINT
2170 PRINT "COMMON RATIO ";
2180 INPUT R
2190 PRINT
2200 PRINT "NUMBER OF TERMS ";
2210 INPUT N
2300 REM %%%%%%%%%%%%%%%%%%%%% CALCULATE AND DISPLAY %%%%%%%%%%%%%%%%%%%%
2310 PRINT
2320 PRINT "THE SEQUENCE:"
2330 PRINT
2340 LET TERM=A
2350 LET SUM=0
2360 FOR I=1 TO N
2370 PRINT TERM;
2380 LET SUM=SUM+TERM
2390 LET TERM=TERM*R
2400 NEXT I
2410 PRINT
2420 PRINT
2430 PRINT "SUM IS ";SUM
2440 PRINT
```

See the Appendix for some general program notes.

```
2500 REM %%%%%%%%%%%%%%%%%%%% ENDING AND ANOTHER GO %%%%%%%%%%%%%%%%%%%%
2510 PRINT " ANOTHER GO?  Y OR N"
2520 GET C$  : REM LET G$=INKEY$
2530 IF C$<>"Y" AND C$<>"N" THEN GOTO 2520
2540 IF C$="Y" THEN GOTO 2110
```

```
GEOMETRIC SEQUENCES

FIRST TERM ? 6

COMMON RATIO ? 0.5

NUMBER OF TERMS ? 5

THE SEQUENCE:

 6   3   1.5   .75   .375


SUM IS   11.625

   ANOTHER GO?  Y OR N
```

Try RUNning the GEOMETRIC SEQUENCES program with the number of terms N very large. You will notice that often you get an OVERFLOW ERROR message. However, if the common ratio R lies between -1 and 1 then an OVERFLOW never occurs. Indeed if we have infinitely many terms in a geometric series and if R is greater than -1 and less than 1 then the sum is A/(1-R). In other words

$$A + A*R + A*R^2 + A*R^3 + A*R^4 + \ldots = A/(1 - R) \quad (\text{if } -1 < R < 1)$$

where "..." means "and so on forever". The reason, briefly, is that R^N becomes smaller and smaller as N gets larger and larger. Two classical examples are given below.

$1 + 1/2 + 1/4 + 1/8 + 1/16 + 1/32 + \ldots = 2 \qquad (A = 1, R = 1/2)$

$1/10 + 1/100 + 1/1000 + 1/10000 + \ldots = 1/9 \qquad (A = 1/10, R = 1/10)$

Snowflakes. An equilateral triangle is a triangle in which all the sides have the same length. Take an equilateral triangle of area 1 square centimetre. This can be used to make a "snowflake" as follows. We add 3 smaller equilateral triangles to this triangle on the middle third of each side. To each of these 12 sides we add smaller equilateral triangles on the middle third of each side.

The process is continued forever. What is the area of the resulting snowflake? Also, what is the perimeter of the snowflake?

To answer this problem first look at how many sides the snowflake has after each step. Initially it has 3 sides. When a triangle is added we obtain 4 sides from each side. Thus at each stage the number of sides is increased four-fold. The number of sides is therefore given by the (geometric) sequence below.

$$3, 3*4, 3*4^2, 3*4^3, 3*4^4, 3*4^5, \ldots$$

Immediately you can see that the number of sides that the final snowflake has is infinitely large.

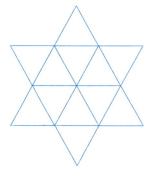

The snowflake is formed by adding a triangle to each side and so the above sequence also gives the number of triangles added at each stage. After the first stage the number of triangles added increases four-fold. The area of each new triangle is one-ninth of the area of the previous triangle. Initially the area is 1. We then add 3 triangles to increase the area by 3/9 = 1/3. From then on there are four times as many triangles being added on each occasion. Hence the area being added at each stage is four-ninths of the previous area added. The total area of the snowflake is therefore given by the following series.

$$1 + 1/3 + (1/3)*(4/9) + (1/3)*(4/9)^2 + (1/3)*(4/9)^3 + \ldots$$

Ignoring the 1 at the beginning, temporarily, we see a geometric series in which the first term is 1/3 and in which the common ratio is 4/9. The sum of this geometric series is equal to $(1/3)/(1 - 4/9)$, in other words 3/5 or 0.6. Hence the total area of our snowflake is 1.6 square centimetres. Even though infinitely many triangles are used to make the snowflake, the area of the snowflake is finite (not infinitely large).

On the other hand the perimeter of the snowflake is infinite. To see this look at each stage in the construction of our snowflake. There are four times as many sides during each stage. But, the side of each new triangle is one-third of the length of the side from which it was made. Thus the perimeter increases by a multiple of four-thirds at each stage. Let L denote the perimeter of the original triangle. At each stage the perimeter of the snowflake is given by the following (geometric) sequence.

$$L, L*(4/3), L*(4/3)^2, L*(4/3)^3, L*(4/3)^4, \ldots$$

You can see that in the end the perimeter will be infinitely large.

The harmonic series. A famous sequence of numbers is the following one.

$$1, 1/2, 1/3, 1/4, 1/5, 1/6, 1/7, 1/8, \ldots$$

It is neither an arithmetic sequence nor a geometric sequence. Adding up the terms of this sequence gives a series which is called the **harmonic series**.

$$1 + 1/2 + 1/3 + 1/4 + 1/5 + 1/6 + 1/7 + 1/8 + \ldots$$

The harmonic series is interesting because the sum is infinitely large - even though the terms being added on get smaller and smaller. You can see this by making the following observations.

> The first term is 1.
> The second term is 1/2.
> The sum of the next 2 terms is bigger than 1/2, since each is bigger than 1/4.
> The sum of the next 4 terms is bigger than 1/2, since each is bigger than 1/8.
> The sum of the next 8 terms is bigger than 1/2, since each is bigger than 1/16.
> And so on.

AND SO ON ... FOREVER

Thus the sum is bigger than 1 + 1/2 + 1/2 + 1/2 + ... , which, as the number of terms increases, gets larger and larger.

You can use the program HARMONIC SERIES to find the sum of any number of terms in the harmonic series. INPUT a number and the sum of this number of terms will be calculated.

HARMONIC SERIES is an independent program which also forms the third part of the program SEQUENCES AND SERIES.

```
3010 REM                    *********************
3020 REM                    *                   *
3030 REM                    * HARMONIC SERIES   *
3040 REM                    *                   *
3050 REM                    *********************
3060 REM
3070 REM
3100 REM %%%%%%%%%%%%%%%%%%%%%% INPUT DATA %%%%%%%%%%%%%%%%%%%%%%%%%
3110 PRINT CHR$(147) : REM CLEAR SCREEN
3120 PRINT "   HARMONIC SERIES"
3130 PRINT
3140 PRINT "1+1/2+1/3+1/4+1/5+..."            See the Appendix for some general
3150 PRINT                                    program notes.
3160 PRINT "NUMBER OF TERMS ";
3170 INPUT N
3180 PRINT
3200 REM %%%%%%%%%%%%%%%%%%%%%% CALCULATE AND DISPLAY %%%%%%%%%%%%%%%%%%%%%%
3210 LET SUM=0
3220 IF N<=0 THEN GOTO 3260
3230 FOR I=1 TO N
3240 LET SUM=SUM+1/I
3250 NEXT I
3260 PRINT "SUM IS ";SUM
3270 PRINT
3500 REM %%%%%%%%%%%%%%%%%%%%%% ENDING AND ANOTHER GO %%%%%%%%%%%%%%%%%%%%%%
3510 PRINT " ANOTHER GO? Y OR N"
3520 GET G$ : REM LET G$=INKEY$
3530 IF G$<>"Y" AND G$<>"N" THEN GOTO 3520
3540 IF G$="Y" THEN GOTO 3150
```

Notice that when calculating the value of SUM in the HARMONIC SERIES program we started with the smallest number and then added on the larger numbers. This is a useful tip whenever adding a lot of numbers together. If you start with the larger numbers first you can easily run into all sorts of round-off errors.

How many terms of the harmonic series do you need in order for the sum to reach 5? How many to reach 10? You could easily use your computer to find out. You need 83 terms to reach 5 and you need 12 367 to reach 10. The number of terms you need to reach 20 is 272 404 867. No doubt you will not bother to check this on your own computer.

```
        HARMONIC SERIES
    1+1/2+1/3+1/4+1/5+...
    NUMBER OF TERMS ? 83
    SUM IS  5.00206828
     ANOTHER GO?  Y OR N
    NUMBER OF TERMS ? 12367
    SUM IS  10.000043
     ANOTHER GO?  Y OR N
```

There is a formula which tells you approximately how many terms you need in order to reach a given sum. Suppose you want to find out how many terms of the harmonic series are needed in order for the sum to be N. Take the number 2.71828 and multiply it by itself N times, then divide the answer by 1.781. The resulting number is the number of terms you need in order to get the sum N. As you can imagine this number increases rapidly as N increases. Indeed it increases exponentially, a phrase often used to describe rapid growth. In fact the number 2.71828 is associated with the exponential function EXP(X) which you have probably already come across on your computer. More will be said about this function later on in the book. If you ask your computer to PRINT EXP(1) you will see the number 2.71828183. Now multiplying this number by itself N times is the same as calculating EXP(N), which your computer can easily do for you. Thus the number of terms in the harmonic series which are needed to produce the sum N is approximately EXP(N)/1.781.

A series, such as the harmonic series, in which the sum is infinitely large is said to be **divergent.** If the sum is finite then it is said to be **convergent.** For example, the geometric series with common ratio between -1 and 1 are convergent.

Caterpillar on elastic. Here is a problem in which the harmonic series arises. A caterpillar is crawling along a piece of elastic trying to get from one end to the other. The caterpillar crawls at the rate of 1 cm/min. The elastic is 7 cm long and can stretch to any length. After a minute you stretch the elastic so that it is twice the original length (making it 14 cm long). The caterpillar holds on tightly to the elastic and is moved along when you stretch the elastic. The caterpillar continues crawling at the same rate. After another minute you stretch the elastic so that it is three times the original length (making it 21 cm long). The caterpillar continues crawling and you continue stretching the elastic every minute, the next time you stretch it to four times the original length. Will the caterpillar ever reach the other end? If so, when?

The answer is that the caterpillar does indeed reach the other end of the elastic in approximately ten and a quarter hours. The caterpillar reaches the end because the harmonic series is divergent! To see this consider what happens. After one minute our caterpillar has crawled 1 cm which is 1/7 of the length of the elastic. When you stretch the elastic the caterpillar is still 1/7 of the way along. During the next minute the caterpillar crawls another centimetre, which is 1/14 of the length of elastic. Thus it has crawled a total of 1/7 + 1/14 of the way along. We rewrite this as (1 + 1/2)/7. You then stretch the elastic to 21 cm and the caterpillar crawls another centimetre, which is 1/21 of the length of elastic. The total amount that the caterpillar has crawled is now

(1 + 1/2 + 1/3)/7

of the way along.

You can see that after N minutes the caterpillar will have crawled

(1 + 1/2 + 1/3 + 1/4 + ... + 1/N)/7

of the way along. The harmonic series is clearly visible here. When N is approximately EXP(7)/1.781 then the value of the above expression is 7/7 and so the caterpillar will have crawled the full length of elastic.

We can ask the same question with any length of elastic; in each case the caterpillar can reach the end. If the length of elastic is 10 cm then it takes the caterpillar more than 8 days to reach the end. If the elastic is a kilometre long (100 000 cm) it will take the caterpillar rather a long time to reach the end. Indeed it will take longer than the estimated age of the universe and the elastic will be longer than the size of the universe. No doubt you and the caterpillar will face some formidable obstacles.

Loving husband? A man walks from his home to work which is one mile away. When he reaches his office he realises that he has forgotten to kiss his wife and so he starts walking back home. Half-way home he changes his mind and decides that he should really go back to work. Having walked 1/3 mile back towards his office he decides that he really is a heel and ought to go and kiss his wife. This time he walks 1/4 mile before he changes his mind again. He continues changing his mind and after the Nth stage he walks 1/N miles before changing his mind. Where does the man end up - apart from "going round the bend"?

The answer is that he ends up 0.6931471806 miles (approximately) away from his home - although it would take him forever to get there. The series that describes his distance from home is given below.

$$1 - 1/2 + 1/3 - 1/4 + 1/5 - 1/6 + 1/7 - 1/8 + \ldots$$

It is called an **alternating series** because the terms alternate in sign. The series is convergent and the sum is approximately 0.6931471806. Write a program to show this.

Series for PI. The number PI is famous and perhaps one of the most remarkable numbers around. It is defined to be the ratio of the circumference of a circle to its diameter. The value of PI accurate to 16 decimal places is 3.1415926535897932. It is approximately 22/7, but it is not equal to 22/7. Already back in 200 BC the Greek mathematician Archimedes (the one that shouted "Eureka" while in his bath) knew that PI was less than 22/7 and greater than 223/71.

The value of PI can be calculated by using a series. There are a number of different series which we shall look at - details of how the series are obtained will not be given.

In about 1673 Gottfried Leibnitz dicovered the following formula for PI.

$$PI = 4 - 4/3 + 4/5 - 4/7 + 4/9 - 4/11 + 4/13 - \ldots$$

However, for calculations, this formula is not very useful. You will need to include many thousands of terms before you get a reasonably accurate approximation to PI.

AND SO ON ... FOREVER

Later on the mathematician Sharp (in about 1699) and Euler (in about 1736) discovered much more useful formulae which are given below.

$$PI = 2*SQR(3)*[1 - 1/(3*3) + 1/(3^2*5) - 1/(3^3*7) + ...]$$
$$PI = SQR(6 + 6/1^2 + 6/2^2 + 6/3^2 + 6/4^2 + 6/5^2 + ...)$$

Your microcomputer probably stores the value of PI in its memory, but it is still interesting to write a program calculating PI using one of the above series. See how many terms of the series you need to obtain a value of PI which is the same as the value stored by your computer.

Some other series. Series crop up all over the place, some further examples will be given.

The sine of an angle is defined geometrically. Draw a circle of radius 1 unit. Measure out the angle A as shown below in the diagram on the left. The vertical height H is called the **sine** of angle A. It is denoted by SIN(A).

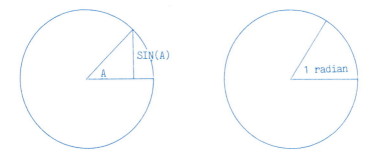

In everyday use angles are measured in degrees and there are 360 degrees in a circle. However your computer (and mathematicians) use **radians.** What is a radian? Measure along the circumference of your circle a distance which is equal to the radius of the circle. The angle subtended by this arc is 1 radian. See the diagram above on the right.

The circumference of a circle of radius 1 unit is 2*PI and so 2*PI radians is the same as 360 degrees. We can therefore convert degrees to radians and vice-versa quite easily with the following formulae.

    A degrees = A*PI/180 radians
    X radians = X*180/PI degrees

Whenever you see SIN(X) in this book, think of X in radians.

The geometric definition of SIN(X) is easy to understand, but it is not very useful for computers. If you type PRINT SIN(0.5) and press RETURN (ENTER or NEW LINE) then the value of SIN(0.5) is displayed. How does your computer know what SIN(X) is? Surely it does not remember the value of SIN(X) for each X, and it certainly does not draw any circles and measure distances. Of course, it uses series. We can calculate SIN(X) by using the following series.

$$SIN(X) = X - X^3/3! + X^5/5! - X^7/7! + X^9/9! - \ldots \quad \text{for } -PI \le X \le PI$$

The notation 3!, 5!, etc., is read "3 factorial", "5 factorial", etc. It means take the product of all the integers from 1 up to that integer. For example 2! = 1*2 = 2, 3! = 1*2*3 = 6, 4! = 1*2*3*4 = 24, and so on. In general factorials are very large. For example, 35! has 40 digits, your microcomputer would probably OVERFLOW if you tried to calculate it. If we did find the answer could we calculate the factorial of that number? The answer, in short, is no! Even if somehow you could calculate it there would not be enough paper in this world to write down the answer. It would take more paper than there is in all the books in all the libraries in the world.

The program CALCULATING SIN(X) illustrates how series can be used to calculate SIN(X). On RUNning the program you INPUT the value of X and the number of terms N that you want to be summed. Notice that usually beyond five or six terms the answer does not change.

CALCULATING SIN(X) is an independent program which forms the fourth part of the program SEQUENCES AND SERIES.

```
4010 REM                   **********************
4020 REM                   *                    *
4030 REM                   * CALCULATING SIN(X) *
4040 REM                   *                    *
4050 REM                   **********************
4060 REM
4070 REM
4100 REM %%%%%%%%%%%%%%%%%%%%% INPUT DATA %%%%%%%%%%%%%%%%%%%%%%%%%%%%%%
4110 PRINT CHR$(147) : REM CLEAR SCREEN
4120 PRINT "  CALCULATING SIN(X)"
4130 PRINT
4140 PRINT " X-X↑3/3!+X↑5/5!-..."
4150 PRINT
4160 PRINT "VALUE OF X ";
4170 INPUT X
4180 PRINT
4190 PRINT "NUMBER OF TERMS ";
4200 INPUT N
```

AND SO ON ... FOREVER

```
4300 REM %%%%%%%%%%%%%%%%%%%% CALCULATE AND DISPLAY %%%%%%%%%%%%%%%%%%%%
4310 LET R=INT(X/π)  : REM π=PI
4320 IF R<0 THEN LET R=R+1
4330 LET Y=X-R*π  : REM π=PI
4340 LET SUM=Y
4350 LET TERM=Y
4360 LET Y=Y*Y
4370 IF N<=0 THEN LET SUM=0
4380 LET M=3
4390 REM %%%%%%%%% LOOP %%%%%%%%%%%%%%%%%%%%%%
4400 IF M>2*N THEN GOTO 4460
4410 LET DENOM=M*(M-1)
4420 LET TERM=-TERM*Y/DENOM
4430 LET SUM=SUM+TERM
4440 LET M=M+2
4450 GOTO 4400
4460 IF INT(R/2)<>R/2 THEN LET SUM=-SUM
4470 PRINT
4480 PRINT "SUM IS ";SUM
4490 PRINT
4500 REM %%%%%%%%%%%%%%%%%%%% ENDING AND ANOTHER GO %%%%%%%%%%%%%%%%%%%%
4510 PRINT " ANOTHER GO?  Y OR N"
4520 GET G$ : REM LET G$=INKEY$
4530 IF G$<>"Y" AND G$<>"N" THEN GOTO 4520
4540 IF G$="Y" THEN GOTO 4150
```

A multiple of PI is subtracted from X until the result lies between 0 and PI.

The sign of SUM is changed if R is odd. This is because of the following formulae.

$SIN(PI + X) = -SIN(X)$
$SIN(2*PI + X) = SIN(X)$

See the Appendix for further notes.

```
         CALCULATING SIN(X)

         X-X↑3/3!+X↑5/5!-...

         VALUE OF X? 0.523599

         NUMBER OF TERMS? 5

         SUM IS   .500000194

          ANOTHER GO?  Y OR N

         VALUE OF X? 0.523599

         NUMBER OF TERMS? 10

         SUM IS   .500000194

          ANOTHER GO?  Y OR N
```

Notice that if X is very small then $X^3/3!$, $X^5/5!$, etc., are extremely small numbers and so SIN(X) is approximately X. You can check this on your computer by calculating SIN(0.01) and SIN(0.001). You can also see this by looking at the geometric definition of SIN(X). For a circle of radius 1 the angle X (in radians) is the arc length, while SIN(X) is the vertical height. For small angles these two lengths are nearly equal.

We have already mentioned that the previous four programs have been numbered so that they may be incorporated into one program entitled SEQUENCES AND SERIES. The following extra lines may be added to enable you to easily use the program of your choice.

```
10 REM                    *************************
20 REM                    *                       *
30 REM                    * SEQUENCES AND SERIES  *
40 REM                    *                       *
50 REM                    *************************
60 REM
70 REM
100 REM %%%%%%%%%%%%%%%%%%%% SETTING UP %%%%%%%%%%%%%%%%%%%%%%%%%%%%%%%
110 PRINT CHR$(147) : REM CLEAR SCREEN
120 PRINT " SEQUENCES AND SERIES"
130 PRINT
140 PRINT "1. ARITHMETIC"
150 PRINT "         SEQUENCES"
160 PRINT
170 PRINT "2. GEOMETRIC"
180 PRINT "         SEQUENCES"
190 PRINT
200 PRINT "3. HARMONIC SERIES"
210 PRINT
220 PRINT "4. CALCULATING SIN(X)"
230 PRINT
240 PRINT "5. END"
250 PRINT
260 PRINT "TYPE NUMBER OF YOUR"
270 PRINT "CHOICE ";
280 INPUT X
290 IF X=5 THEN END : REM STOP
300 IF X<1 OR X>4 THEN GOTO 260
310 ON X GOTO 1110,2110,3110,4110
320 REM GOTO 110+X*1000

1550 GOTO 110
2550 GOTO 110
3550 GOTO 110
4550 GOTO 110
```

See the Appendix for some general program notes.

```
         SEQUENCES AND SERIES

       1.  ARITHMETIC
                    SEQUENCES

       2.  GEOMETRIC
                    SEQUENCES

       3.  HARMONIC SERIES

       4.  CALCULATING SIN(X)

       5.  END

       TYPE NUMBER OF YOUR
       CHOICE ? 2
```

The exponential function was briefly mentioned earlier on. As a series it takes the following form.

$$EXP(X) = 1 + X + X^2/2! + X^3/3! + X^4/4! + X^5/5! + \ldots$$

Why not write a program for EXP(X) similar to CALCULATING SIN(X) and add it to the program SEQUENCES AND SERIES?

Some further series are given below. You might like to use them to write some programs and add them to SEQUENCES AND SERIES.

$$COS(X) = 1 - X^2/2! + X^4/4! - X^6/6! + X^8/8! - \ldots$$
$$ATN(X) = X - X^3/3 + X^5/5 - X^7/7 + X^9/9 - \ldots \quad \text{provided } -1 < X < 1$$
$$LN(X) = 2*(Y + Y^3/3 + Y^5/5 + Y^7/7 + \ldots) \quad \text{where } Y = (X - 1)/(X + 1)$$

Note that ATN(X) denotes the arctangent of X, some computers use ATAN(X). Also note that LN(X) denotes the natural logarithm of X which some microcomputers denote by LOG(X).

Intelligence Tests. A popular question in intelligence tests and quizzes involves a sequence of numbers or letters. For example,

    15, 12, 9, 6   or   L, J, H, F

You are then asked to write down the next term in the sequence. Your microcomputer can be used to set up all sorts of sequences to create interesting games. Such sequences have been used in the program INTELLIGENCE TESTS. The program involves quite a number of different sequences which are randomly selected.

No time limit has been put on the test. This is something you could include yourself.

```
10 REM                   *********************
20 REM                   *                   *
30 REM                   * INTELLIGENCE TEST *
40 REM                   *                   *
50 REM                   *********************
60 REM
70 REM
100 REM %%%%%%%%%%%%%%%%%%%% SETTING UP %%%%%%%%%%%%%%%%%%%%%%%%%%%%%
110 LET J=1                              J is a counter for the number of
120 LET SC=0
130 LET S=ASC("A") : REM LET S=CODE("A") turns. SC is the score.
140 GOTO 290
200 REM %%%%%%%%%%%%%%%%%%% THE MAIN LOOP %%%%%%%%%%%%%%%%%%%%%%%%%%
210 IF J>10 THEN GOTO 710
220 PRINT
230 PRINT
240 PRINT "   PRESS Y TO GO ON"
250 PRINT
260 GET G$ : REM LET G$=INKEY$
270 IF G$<>"Y" THEN GOTO 260
280 REM %%%%%%%% RANDOM NUMBERS %%%%%%%%%%%
290 LET A=INT(RND(1)*10+1)
300 LET N=INT(RND(1)*4)                  A, N, B, C are various random
310 LET B=INT(RND(1)*10)                 numbers used in the sequences.
320 LET C=1
330 IF RND(1)<.5 THEN LET C=-1
340 PRINT CHR$(147) : REM CLEAR SCREEN
350 PRINT "   INTELLIGENCE TEST"
360 PRINT "     SEQUENCE ";J
370 PRINT
380 PRINT "WHAT IS THE NEXT TERM?"
390 REM %%%%%%%% SEQUENCE CHOICE %%%%%%%%%%
400 ON INT(RND(1)*8)+1 GOSUB 1110,1310,1510,1710,1910,2110,2310,2510
410 REM GOSUB 1110+200*INT(RND*8)        Line 400 selects the sequence.
420 PRINT
430 LET J=J+1                            Sinclair users should use line
440 INPUT Y$                             410.
450 IF Y$=X$ OR " "+Y$=X$ THEN GOTO 560
```

AND SO ON ... FOREVER

```
460 GOSUB 911 : REM NOISE FOR ERROR
470 PRINT
480 PRINT "   NO - TRY AGAIN"
490 PRINT
500 INPUT Y$
510 IF Y$=X$ OR " "+Y$=X$ THEN GOTO 560
520 GOSUB 911 : REM NOISE FOR ERROR
530 PRINT
540 PRINT "THE ANSWER IS ";X$
550 GOTO 210
560 GOSUB 921 : REM WELL DONE NOISE
570 PRINT
580 PRINT "   WELL DONE"
590 LET SC=SC+1
600 GOTO 210
700 REM %%%%%%%%%%%%%%%%%%%%% ENDING %%%%%%%%%%%%%%%%%%%%%%%%%%%%%%%%%%
710 PRINT
720 PRINT
730 PRINT "YOUR SCORE OUT OF 10"
740 PRINT
750 PRINT "IS   ";SC
760 GOSUB 931 : REM SCORE NOISE
770 PRINT
780 PRINT
790 PRINT " ANOTHER GO? Y OR N"
800 GET G$ : REM LET G$=INKEY$
810 IF G$<>"Y" AND G$<>"N" THEN GOTO 800
820 IF G$="Y" THEN GOTO 110
830 END : REM STOP
900 REM %%%%%%%%%%%%%%%%%%%%% SOUND EFFECTS %%%%%%%%%%%%%%%%%%%%%%%%%%%
910 REM %%%%%%%%%%%%%%%%%%%%% ERROR NOISE %
911 POKE 36879,26+RND(1)*6
912 POKE 36878,15
913 T=150:GOSUB 941:T=130:GOSUB 941
914 POKE 36878,0
915 RETURN
920 REM %%%%%%%%%%%%%%%%%%%%% WELL DONE NOISE
921 POKE 36879,26+RND(1)*6
922 POKE 36878,15
923 T=220:GOSUB 941:T=200:GOSUB 941
924 T=220:GOSUB 941
925 POKE 36878,0
926 RETURN
930 REM %%%%%%%%%%%%%%%%%%%%% SCORE NOISE %
931 POKE 36878,15
932 FOR K=1 TO SC
933 POKE 36879,26+RND(1)*6
934 T=220:GOSUB 941:T=0:GOSUB 941
935 NEXT K
936 POKE 36878,0:RETURN
940 REM %%%%%%%%%%%%%%%%%%%%% THE NOISE %%%
941 POKE 36876,T+J
942 FOR I=1 TO 125:NEXT I
943 POKE 36876,0
944 RETURN
```

You have two tries to get the correct answer.

This prints your score out of 10 and asks whether you want another go.

Put your own sound effects here. Three different sound effects are recommended. The first is used to indicate an incorrect answer. The second is used to indicate a correct answer and the third is used to indicate the score.

```
1000 REM %%%%%%%%%%%%%%%%%%%% SUBROUTINES %%%%%%%%%%%%%%%%%%%%%%%%%%
1100 REM %%%%%%% ARITHMETIC %%%%%%%%%%%%%%%
1110 IF C<0 THEN LET B=B+80+INT(RND(1)*10)
1120 FOR I=1 TO 6
1130 PRINT STR$(A*I*C+B); : REM PRINT " ";A*I*C+B;
1140 NEXT I
1150 LET X$=STR$(A*I*C+B)
1160 PRINT
1170 RETURN
1300 REM %%%%%%% ARITHMETIC LETTERS %%%%%%
1310 FOR I=N TO N+6
1320 LET W=A*C*I+B
1330 LET W=W+S-26*INT(W/26)
1340 PRINT " ";CHR$(W);
1350 NEXT I
1360 LET W=A*C*I+B
1370 LET W=W+S-26*INT(W/26)
1380 LET X$=CHR$(W)
1390 PRINT
1400 RETURN
1500 REM %%%%%%% GEOMETRIC %%%%%%%%%%%%%%%%
1510 LET W=1
1520 LET N=N+2
1530 FOR I=1 TO 4
1540 LET W=W*N
1550 PRINT STR$(W+A); : REM PRINT " ";W+A;
1560 NEXT I
1570 LET X$=STR$(W*N+A)
1580 PRINT
1590 RETURN
1700 REM %%%%%%% FIBONACCI %%%%%%%%%%%%%%%%
1710 PRINT STR$(B);STR$(A); : REM PRINT " ";B;" ";A;
1720 PRINT STR$(B+A);STR$(B+2*A); : REM PRINT " ";B+A;" ";B+2*A;
1730 PRINT STR$(2*B+3*A);STR$(3*B+5*A):REM PRINT " ";2*B+3*A;" ";3*B+5*A
1740 LET X$=STR$(5*B+8*A)
1750 RETURN
1900 REM %%%%%%% FACTORIALS %%%%%%%%%%%%%%%
1910 LET W=A
1920 PRINT STR$(W+C); : REM PRINT " ";W+C;
1930 FOR I=1 TO 4
1940 LET W=W*I
1950 PRINT STR$(W+C); : REM PRINT " ";W+C;
1960 NEXT I
1970 PRINT
1980 LET X$=STR$(5*W+C)
1990 RETURN
2100 REM %%%%%%% ARITHMETIC MIXED %%%%%%%%%
2110 FOR I=N TO N+6
2120 LET W=A*C*I+B
2130 LET W=W+S-26*INT(W/26)
2140 LET Y$=" "+CHR$(W)
2150 IF 2*INT(I/2)=I THEN LET Y$=STR$(W-S+1) : REM Y$=" "+STR$(W-S+1)
2160 PRINT Y$;
2170 NEXT I
2180 LET W=A*C*I+B
2190 LET W=W+S-26*INT(W/26)
```

Some computers print a space before and after a number, some do not. If yours does not then you may find that the PRINT statements following the REMarks give a better display.

The REMarks may be safely omitted.

```
2200 LET X$=CHR$(W)
2210 IF 2*INT(I/2)=I THEN LET X$=STR$(W-S+1)
2220 PRINT
2230 RETURN
2300 REM %%%%%%%% TWO ARITHMETIC %%%%%%%%%%
2310 LET W=80+INT(RND(1)*10)
2320 FOR I=1 TO 6
2330 PRINT STR$(W); : REM PRINT " ";W;
2340 LET W=W+C*A
2350 LET C=-C
2360 LET A=A+B+1
2370 NEXT I
2380 PRINT
2390 LET X$=STR$(W)
2400 RETURN
2500 REM %%%%%%%% INCREASING ARITHMETIC %%%
2510 LET W=85+INT(RND(1)*10)
2520 LET D=1
2530 IF RND(1)<.5 THEN LET D=-1
2540 FOR I=1 TO 6
2550 PRINT STR$(W); : REM PRINT " ";W;
2560 LET W=W+C*A
2570 LET C=C*D
2580 LET A=A+I
2590 NEXT I
2600 PRINT
2610 LET X$=STR$(W)
2620 RETURN
```

See the Appendix for further notes

```
        INTELLIGENCE TEST
           SEQUENCE   1

     WHAT IS THE NEXT TERM?

       81  77  85  73  89  69

     ? 93

          WELL DONE


          PRESS Y TO GO ON
```

```
        INTELLIGENCE TEST
           SEQUENCE  9

   WHAT IS THE NEXT TERM?

    16 G 24 O 6 W 14

   ? Y

       NO - TRY AGAIN

   ? Z

   THE ANSWER IS E


       PRESS Y TO GO ON
```

```
        INTELLIGENCE TEST
           SEQUENCE  10

   WHAT IS THE NEXT TERM?

    7 7 15 47 191

   ? 959

        WELL DONE


   YOUR SCORE OUT OF 10

   IS     9

     ANOTHER GO?  Y OR N
```

UP AND DOWN, ROUND AND ROUND
about functions, graphs and polar coordinates

The area A of a circle of radius R is given by the formula A = PI*R*R. Each value of R determines a value of A. We say that A is a **function** of R.

You have probably seen expressions like

   Y = X*X, Y = SIN(X), Y = SQR(X), Y = SQR(X*X + 2), ...

These are all examples of functions. In each case Y is a function of X. Input a value of X and the output is a value of Y. Notice that for some functions you cannot input every value of X. For example, you cannot input a negative number in SQR(X).

The actual symbols used are not important. For example, each of the following represents the same function.

   B = A*A, W = U*U, Y = X*X

In each case the function evaluates the square of a number. Usually we use the symbols Y and X.

A formula for a function, by itself, may not be very illuminating. For example, look at Y = X*X*SIN(1/X). How does this function behave when X is large? What about when X is small? "A picture is worth a thousand words" and so to help us understand functions we often draw a "picture" or graph of the function.

Graphs and coordinates. A point in the plane (or on the screen of your computer display) is usually represented by a pair of numbers (X,Y). This pair tells you the distance your point is from some axes. The number X gives the horizontal distance while Y gives the vertical distance. Conventionally the distance X is measured horizontally from left to right, while

Y is measured vertically upwards from the axis. A negative number is measured in the opposite direction. See the diagram below.

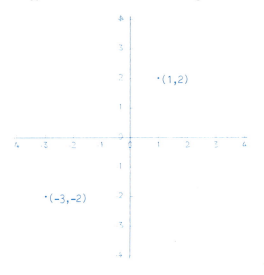

The pair (X,Y) is called the **cartesian coordinates** or just **coordinates** of the point. The name cartesian coordinates is in honour of the French mathematician René "I think, therefore I am" Descartes (1596-1650) who is given credit for this method of describing the position of a point.

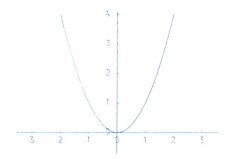

Plotting the **graph** of a function means that for each value of X, in some specified range, you calculate the corresponding value of Y and place (plot) a point at the coordinates (X,Y). For example, the graph of Y = X*X is shown here on the left.

An interesting function to look at is Y = X*X*SIN(1/X). The graph of this function, plotted over four different ranges of X, appears on the opposite page. If you plot the graph for X in the range between -10 and 10 then the graph looks very much like a straight line drawn with a ruler (see Frame 1 on the opposite page). However, it looks as if the ruler slipped when the line was being drawn near X=0. But of course this is where something interesting is going on. The next frame (Frame 2) zooms in and plots the graph for X between -1 and 1. This graph begins to show what is happening near X=0. Frames 3 and 4 continue zooming in by looking at the ranges -0.1 to 0.1 and -0.025 to 0.025 respectively.

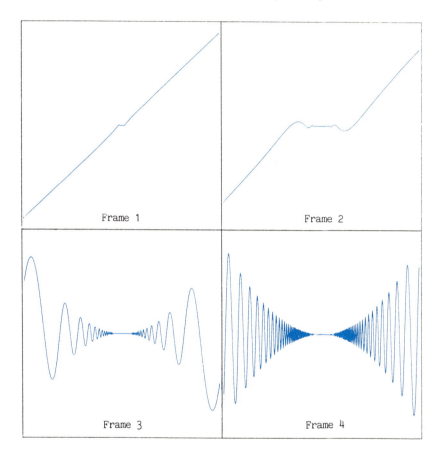

Graphs of the function Y = X*X*SIN(1/X)

Why does the graph of X*X*SIN(1/X) look like a straight line when X is large? To answer this we rewrite the function as X*SIN(1/X)/(1/X) and denote 1/X by U. Our function becomes X*SIN(U)/U. Now when X is large 1/X (in other words U) is small. But recall that when U is small SIN(U)/U is approximately 1 and so X*SIN(U)/U is approximately X. Thus when X is large we are plotting, approximately, the graph of Y = X, which is a straight line.

When you look at the graphs for small values of X you may notice something interesting (especially if you squint your eyes). The highest points on the graph look like the graph of X*X, the lowest points look like the graph of -X*X and the rest of the graph runs up and down between these points. The reason for this is that as X goes towards 0 it passes through the numbers -1/PI, -1/(2*PI), -1/(3*PI), and so on. At such times SIN(1/X) is either 1 or -1, and so X*X*SIN(1/X) becomes X*X or -X*X.

Your microcomputer can be used in a very effective way to display graphs of functions. And more, you can use your computer to "zoom in" on any interesting looking parts and learn something about the function. Even the graphics on a ZX 81 reveal a surprising amount.

With the program GRAPH PLOTTING you can investigate the graphs of functions over any range you like. You can look at the graphs "globally", that is over a large range of X, or you can zoom in and investigate the graph "locally" over a small range of X.

The BASIC on computers varies from one machine to another and writing a general program is quite hard. When it comes to a graphics program the situation is almost impossible. Some microcomputers have PLOT and DRAW facilities while many do not. The latter rely upon POKEing to achieve graphics and this is very machine dependent. The program GRAPH PLOTTING has been written in such a way as to aid adapting it for your personal computer.

One of the first things to do is to find out the resolution of your screen in terms of pixels or points that can be plotted. For example, the ZX 81 has a resolution of 64 pixels horizontally and 44 vertically while the ZX Spectrum has 256 by 176 pixels. These numbers, less 1 or 2, are called SX and SY respectively in the GRAPH PLOTTING program. See the diagram on the opposite page.

To help you adapt GRAPH PLOTTING for your computer two extra listings are provided. The program SINCLAIR GRAPH PLOTTING is included to illustrate how the program GRAPH PLOTTING is adapted for a microcomputer with a PLOT facility. The VIC 20 GRAPH PLOTTING program shows how to adapt GRAPH PLOTTING for a microcomputer without PLOT in its BASIC. For some extra comments see the Appendix.

UP AND DOWN, ROUND AND ROUND

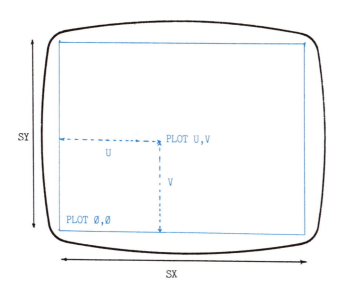

```
10 REM
20 REM                   ********************
30 REM                   *                  *
40 REM                   *  GRAPH PLOTTING  *
50 REM                   *                  *
60 REM                   ********************
70 REM
100 REM ///////////////////// SETTING UP /////////////////////////////////
110 LET CS$=CHR$(147) : REM CODE FOR CLEAR SCREEN
120 LET SX=176 : REM SCREEN SIZE HORIZ
130 LET SY=160 : REM SCREEN SIZE VERT
140 LET HY=SY/2
150 PRINT CS$ : REM CLS
160 PRINT "    GRAPH PLOTTING"
170 PRINT
180 PRINT "1.Y = X*X*SIN(1/X)"
190 PRINT
200 PRINT "2.Y = X*SIN(1/X)"
210 PRINT
220 PRINT "3.Y = SQR(X*X+2)"
230 PRINT
240 PRINT "4.Y =COS(X*EXP(-X/5))"
250 PRINT
260 PRINT "5.Y = 6+2*X*X-X*X*X*X"
270 PRINT
280 PRINT "TYPE IN THE NUMBER OF"
290 PRINT "THE EQUATION";
300 INPUT N
310 IF N=1 THEN DEF FNA(X)=X*X*SIN(1/X)
320 IF N=2 THEN DEF FNA(X)=X*SIN(1/X)
```

SX and SY denote the number of points that can be plotted on the screen. Put in the values appropriate for your computer.

```
330 IF N=3 THEN DEF FNA(X)=SQR(X*X+2)
340 IF N=4 THEN DEF FNA(X)=COS(X*EXP(-X/5))
350 IF N=5 THEN DEF FNA(X)=6+2*X*X-X*X*X*X
360 PRINT
370 PRINT "VALUES OF X FOR PLOT"
380 PRINT
390 PRINT "LOWEST VALUE";
400 INPUT A
410 PRINT
420 PRINT "HIGHEST VALUE";
430 INPUT B
440 PRINT
450 IF A>=B THEN PRINT "ERROR - TRY AGAIN"
460 IF A>=B THEN GOTO 360
500 REM %%%%%%%%%%%%%%%%%%%%% CALCULATING RANGE OF Y %%%%%%%%%%%%%%%%%%%%
510 PRINT "CALCULATING RANGE OF Y"
520 LET C=(B-A)/100
530 LET M=1.0E-30
540 FOR X=A TO B STEP C
550 IF X=0 THEN GOTO 580
560 LET Y=ABS(FNA(X))
570 IF M<Y THEN LET M=Y
580 NEXT X
590 PRINT "READY FOR PLOTTING"
600 FOR I=1 TO 1000
610 NEXT I
620 PRINT CS$ : REM CLS
630 GOSUB 1010 : REM PREPARE SCREEN IF NECESSARY
700 REM %%%%%%%%%%%%%%%%%%%%% PLOTTING %%%%%%%%%%%%%%%%%%%%%%%%%%%%%
710 LET C=C/10 : REM TRY C/5 OR C/20
720 FOR X=A TO B STEP C
730 IF X=0 THEN GOTO 790
740 LET Y=FNA(X)
750 LET U=SX*(X-A)/(B-A)
760 LET V=HY+HY*Y/M
770 IF V<0 OR V>SY THEN GOTO 790
780 GOSUB 1110 : REM PLOT U,V
790 NEXT X
800 REM %%%%%%%%%%%%%%%%%%%%% ENDING AND ANOTHER GO %%%%%%%%%%%%%%%%%%%%
810 GET G$ : REM LET G$=INKEY$
820 IF G$="" THEN GOTO 810
830 GOSUB 1210 : REM RESTORE SCREEN IF NECESSARY
840 PRINT CS$ : REM CLS
850 PRINT " ANOTHER GO?  Y OR N"
860 GET G$ : REM LET G$=INKEY$
870 IF G$<>"Y" AND G$<>"N" THEN GOTO 860
880 IF G$="Y" THEN GOTO 150
890 END : REM STOP

1000 REM %%%%%%%%%%%%%%%%%%%%% PREPARE HI-RES SCREEN %%%%%%%%%%%%%%%%%%%%
1010 RETURN
1100 REM %%%%%%%%%%%%%%%%%%%%% PLOT VIA POKE %%%%%%%%%%%%%%%%%%%%%%%%%%%%
1110 RETURN
1200 REM %%%%%%%%%%%%%%%%%%%%% RESTORE SCREEN %%%%%%%%%%%%%%%%%%%%%%%%%%%
1210 RETURN
```

This part calculates the range of Y (approximately, to save time). The graph is then scaled to fill your screen.

This PLOTs the graph. A check is made to ensure that only the points that will fit on the screen are plotted.

UP AND DOWN, ROUND AND ROUND

```
         GRAPH PLOTTING
1. Y = X*X*SIN(1/X)
2. Y = X*SIN(1/X)
3. Y = SQR(X*X+2)
4. Y =COS(X*EXP(-X/5))
5. Y = 6+2*X*X-X*X*X*X
TYPE IN THE NUMBER OF
THE EQUATION? 1
VALUES OF X FOR PLOT
LOWEST VALUE? -0.1
HIGHEST VALUE? 0.1
CALCULATING RANGE OF Y
```

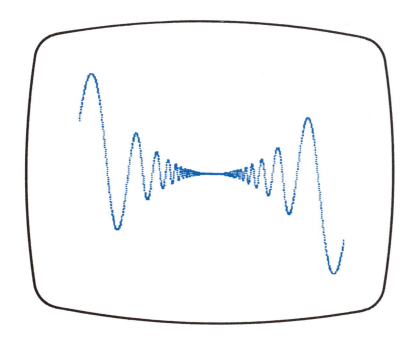

UP AND DOWN, ROUND AND ROUND

```
 10 REM                  *******************
 20 REM                  *     SINCLAIR    *
 30 REM                  *  GRAPH PLOTTING *
 40 REM                  *                 *
 50 REM                  *******************
 60 REM
 70 REM
100 REM %%%%%%%%%%%%%%%%%%%%% SETTING UP %%%%%%%%%%%%%%%%%%%%%%%%%%%%%%
120 LET SX=62
130 LET SY=42
140 LET HY=SY/2
150 CLS
160 PRINT "    GRAPH PLOTTING"
170 PRINT
180 PRINT "1.Y = X*X*SIN(1/X)"
190 PRINT
200 PRINT "2.Y = X*SIN(1/X)"
210 PRINT
220 PRINT "3.Y = SQR(X*X+2)"
230 PRINT
240 PRINT "4.Y =COS(X*EXP(-X/5))"
250 PRINT
260 PRINT "5.Y = 6+2*X*X-X*X*X*X"
270 PRINT
280 PRINT "TYPE IN THE NUMBER OF"
290 PRINT "THE EQUATION ";
300 INPUT N
305 PRINT N
310 IF N=1 THEN LET A$="X*X*SIN(1/X)"
320 IF N=2 THEN LET A$="X*SIN(1/X)"
330 IF N=3 THEN LET A$="SQR(X*X+2)"
340 IF N=4 THEN LET A$="COS(X*EXP(-X/5))"
350 IF N=5 THEN LET A$="6+2*X*X-X*X*X*X"
360 PRINT
370 PRINT "VALUES OF X FOR PLOT"
380 PRINT
390 PRINT "LOWEST VALUE ";
400 INPUT A
405 PRINT A
410 PRINT
420 PRINT "HIGHEST VALUE ";
430 INPUT B
435 PRINT B
440 PRINT
450 IF A>=B THEN PRINT "ERROR - TRY AGAIN"
460 IF A>=B THEN GOTO 360
500 REM %%%%%%%%%%%%%%%%%%%% CALCULATING RANGE OF Y %%%%%%%%%%%%%%%%%%
510 PRINT "CALCULATING RANGE OF Y"
520 LET C=(B-A)/100
530 LET M=1.0E-30
535 REM FAST FOR ZX81
540 FOR X=A TO B STEP C
550 IF X=0 THEN GOTO 580
560 LET Y=ABS(VAL(A$))
570 IF M<Y THEN LET M=Y
580 NEXT X
585 REM SLOW FOR ZX81
590 PRINT "READY FOR PLOTTING"
600 FOR I=1 TO 100
```

SX and SY denote the number of points that can be plotted on the screen. Put in the values appropriate for your computer. For the ZX Spectrum use

SX = 255, SY = 175

This part calculates the range of Y (approximately, to save time). The graph is then scaled to fill your screen.

```
610 NEXT I
620 CLS
700 REM %%%%%%%%%%%%%%%%%%%% PLOTTING %%%%%%%%%%%%%%%%%%%%%%%%%%%%%%
710 LET C=C/10 : REM TRY C/5 OR C/20
720 FOR X=A TO B STEP C
730 IF X=0 THEN GOTO 790
740 LET Y=VAL(A$)
750 LET U=SX*(X-A)/(B-A)
760 LET V=HY+HY*Y/M
770 IF V<0 OR V>SY THEN GOTO 790
780 PLOT U,V
790 NEXT X
800 REM %%%%%%%%%%%%%%%%%%%% ENDING AND ANOTHER GO %%%%%%%%%%%%%%%%%%%%
810 LET G$=INKEY$
820 IF G$="" THEN GOTO 810
850 PRINT " ANOTHER GO?  Y OR N"
860 LET G$=INKEY$
870 IF G$<>"Y" AND G$<>"N" THEN GOTO 860
880 IF G$="Y" THEN GOTO 150
890 STOP
```

This PLOTs the graph. A check is made to ensure that only the points that will fit on the screen are plotted.

```
10 REM                  ********************
20 REM                  *      VIC 20      *
30 REM                  *  GRAPH PLOTTING  *
40 REM                  *                  *
50 REM                  ********************
60 REM
70 REM
100 REM %%%%%%%%%%%%%%%%%%%% SETTING UP %%%%%%%%%%%%%%%%%%%%%%%%%%%%
110 LET CS$=CHR$(147) : REM CODE FOR CLEAR SCREEN
120 LET SX=176 : REM SCREEN SIZE HORIZ
130 LET SY=160 : REM SCREEN SIZE VERT
140 LET HY=SY/2
145 GOSUB 1310 : REM EXTRA SETTINGS
150 PRINT CS$
160 PRINT "    GRAPH PLOTTING"
170 PRINT
180 PRINT "1.Y = X*X*SIN(1/X)"
190 PRINT
200 PRINT "2.Y = X*SIN(1/X)"
210 PRINT
220 PRINT "3.Y = SQR(X*X+2)"
230 PRINT
240 PRINT "4.Y =COS(X*EXP(-X/5))"
250 PRINT
260 PRINT "5.Y = 6+2*X*X-X*X*X*X"
270 PRINT
280 PRINT "TYPE IN THE NUMBER OF"
290 PRINT "THE EQUATION";
300 INPUT N
310 IF N=1 THEN DEF FNA(X)=X*X*SIN(1/X)
320 IF N=2 THEN DEF FNA(X)=X*SIN(1/X)
330 IF N=3 THEN DEF FNA(X)=SQR(X*X+2)
340 IF N=4 THEN DEF FNA(X)=COS(X*EXP(-X/5))
350 IF N=5 THEN DEF FNA(X)=6+2*X*X-X*X*X*X
360 PRINT
370 PRINT "VALUES OF X FOR PLOT"
```

SX and SY denote the number of points that can be plotted on the screen. Put in the values appropriate for your computer.

```
380 PRINT
390 PRINT "LOWEST VALUE";
400 INPUT A
410 PRINT
420 PRINT "HIGHEST VALUE";
430 INPUT B
440 PRINT
450 IF A>=B THEN PRINT "ERROR - TRY AGAIN"
460 IF A>=B THEN GOTO 360
500 REM %%%%%%%%%%%%%%%%%%%% CALCULATING RANGE OF Y %%%%%%%%%%%%%%%%%%%%
510 PRINT "CALCULATING RANGE OF Y"
520 LET C=(B-A)/100
530 LET M=1.0E-30
540 FOR X=A TO B STEP C
550 IF X=0 THEN GOTO 580
560 LET Y=ABS(FNA(X))
570 IF M<Y THEN LET M=Y
580 NEXT X
590 PRINT "READY FOR PLOTTING"
600 FOR I=1 TO 1000
610 NEXT I
620 PRINT CS$
630 GOSUB 1010 : REM PREPARE SCREEN
700 REM %%%%%%%%%%%%%%%%%%%% PLOTTING %%%%%%%%%%%%%%%%%%%%%%%%%%%%%%
710 LET C=C/10 : REM TRY C/5 OR C/20
720 FOR X=A TO B STEP C
730 IF X=0 THEN GOTO 790
740 LET Y=FNA(X)
750 LET U=SX*(X-A)/(B-A)
760 LET V=HY+HY*Y/M
770 IF V<0 OR V>SY THEN GOTO 790
780 GOSUB 1110 : REM PLOT U,V
790 NEXT X
800 REM %%%%%%%%%%%%%%%%%%%% ENDING AND ANOTHER GO %%%%%%%%%%%%%%%%%%%%
810 GET G$ : REM LET G$=INKEY$
820 IF G$="" THEN GOTO 810
830 GOSUB 1210 : REM RESTORE SCREEN
840 PRINT CS$
850 PRINT " ANOTHER GO?  Y OR N"
860 GET G$ : REM LET G$=INKEY$
870 IF G$<>"Y" AND G$<>"N" THEN GOTO 860
880 IF G$="Y" THEN GOTO 150
890 END : REM STOP
1000 REM %%%%%%%%%%%%%%%%%%%% PREPARE HI-RES SCREEN %%%%%%%%%%%%%%%%%%%%
1010 POKE 36869,RB+12:POKE 36867,(PEEK(36867) AND 128) OR 21
1020 FOR I=RR TO SS:POKE I,0:NEXT I
1030 FOR I=0 TO 219:POKE PP+I,I-32*Q:POKE QQ+I,2:NEXT I
1040 RETURN
1100 REM %%%%%%%%%%%%%%%%%%%% PLOT VIA POKE %%%%%%%%%%%%%%%%%%%%
1110 V=SY-V
1120 J=INT(U/8)
1130 L=INT(U-8*J)
1140 I=INT(V/16)
1150 K=INT(V-16*I)
1160 W=RR+I*352+J*16+K
1170 POKE W,PEEK(W) OR 2↑(7-L)
1180 RETURN
```

This part calculates the range of Y (approximately, to save time). The graph is then scaled to fill your screen.

This PLOTs the graph. A check is made to ensure that only the points that will fit on the screen are plotted.

Use the appropriate POKEs for your microcomputer.

```
1200 REM %%%%%%%%%%%%%%%%%%%%%% RESTORE SCREEN %%%%%%%%%%%%%%%%%%%%%%%%%
1210 POKE 36869,R8:POKE 36867,R6:POKE 198,0
1220 RETURN
1300 REM %%%%%%%%%%%%%%%%%%%%%% VIC 20 SETTINGS %%%%%%%%%%%%%%%%%%%%%%%%
1310 Q=PEEK(44)>=18:PP=7680+Q*3584:QQ=38400+Q*512
1320 IFQ=-1ANDPEEK(44)<32THEN PRINT "PROGRAM ABORTED - SEE APPENDIX":END
1330 RR=4096-Q*512:SS=RR+3583:R8=PEEK(36869):R6=PEEK(36867)
1340 RETURN
```

Experiment with the function X*X*SIN(1/X) initially. After that try some of the other functions in the program. You may also like to include some of the following functions into your program.

$$Y = SQR(X*X + 2)*SIN(X)$$
$$Y = X*SIN(1/X)*SIN(1/X)$$
$$Y = COS(X*EXP(-X/5))*SIN(X)$$
$$Y = SIN(X/LN(ABS(X) + 1.1))$$

Polar coordinates. Points in the plane are usually represented by cartesian coordinates. There is another way of locating points in the plane - this is by **polar coordinates.** Here we have one axis and a point on it

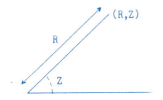

called the **pole**. A point is now represented by a pair of numbers (R,Z) where R is the distance to the pole and Z is the angle between the axis and the line from the pole to this point - this angle being measured anticlockwise.

It is convenient to allow R and Z to be negative. In that case the measurements are made in the opposite direction. Thus, for example, the following each represent the <u>same</u> point.

(2,PI/2)   (2,-3*PI/2)   (-2,-PI/2)

Polar bees. Honey bees use polar coordinates to communicate information about sources of food. Having found a new source of food (a flower bed) a scout bee returns to the hive, gives a sample of the food and performs a dance to show where the food is. This dance consists of running in a straight line waggling from side to side and then circling back. The straight run is repeated but this time the circling back is performed in the opposite direction. The whole process is repeated several times. The length of the straight run indicates how far away the flower bed is. The direction of this straight run gives the direction of the flower bed. Thus the scout bee tells the others the polar coordinates of the new source of food.

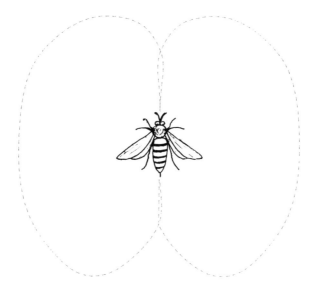

Polar graphs. A function that involves polar coordinates (R,Z) is called a **polar function.** For example, R = SIN(Z) is a polar function. You can draw graphs of polar functions. This time, for each value of Z, in some specified range, you plot the point (R,Z) using polar coordinates. To make the plotting easier we revert back to cartesian coordinates. The point (R,Z) in polar coordinates is the same as the point (R*COS(Z),R*SIN(Z)) in cartesian coordinates, and this is what we plot. The graph of the polar function R = SIN(Z) is very different from the graph of the ordinary function Y = SIN(X). In fact it is a circle.

There are many beautiful curves that can be described simply by polar coordinates. Here are some examples.

```
R = 1                a circle
R = SIN(2*Z)         a four-leaved rose
R = SIN(7*Z)         a seven-leaved rose
R = 1 + 2*COS(Z)     a limacon
R = 1 + COS(Z)       a cardioid
R = Z/4              a spiral
R = 1 + SIN(2*Z)     a two-leaved rose
R = 1 + 2*COS(2*Z)   looping the loop
```

UP AND DOWN, ROUND AND ROUND

Graphs of some of these polar functions appear on this and the next page.

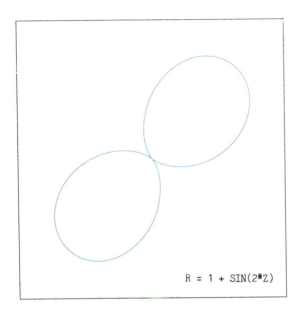

R = 1 + SIN(2*Z)

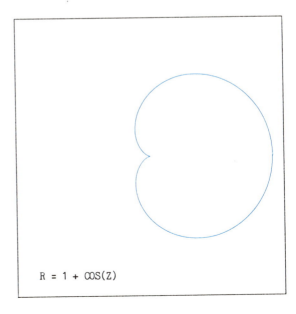

R = 1 + COS(Z)

R = 1 + 2*COS(2*Z)

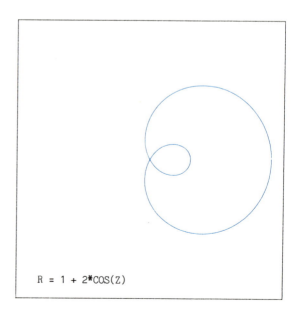

R = 1 + 2*COS(Z)

UP AND DOWN, ROUND AND ROUND

The program POLAR GRAPHICS, which is an adaptation of the GRAPH PLOTTING program, enables you to plot the graphs of polar functions. It has a library of several different polar functions which you can experiment with. A version for Sinclair microcomputers is also included.

```
10 REM                  *******************
20 REM                  *                 *
30 REM                  * POLAR GRAPHICS  *
40 REM                  *                 *
50 REM                  *******************
60 REM
70 REM
100 REM %%%%%%%%%%%%%%%%%%%%% SETTING UP %%%%%%%%%%%%%%%%%%%%%%%%%%%%%
110 LET CS$=CHR$(147) : REM CODE FOR CLEAR SCREEN
120 LET SX=144 : REM SCREEN SIZE HORIZ
130 LET SY=176 : REM SCREEN SIZE VERT
140 LET RATIO=0.6 : REM TO MAKE HORIZ & VERT LINES SAME LENGTH
150 LET HY=SY/2
160 LET HX=SX/2
165 GOSUB 1310 : REM EXTRA VIC 20 SETTINGS
170 PRINT CS$ : REM CLS
180 PRINT "   POLAR GRAPHICS"
190 PRINT
200 PRINT "1. R = 1"
210 PRINT
220 PRINT "2. R = SIN(2*Z)"
230 PRINT
240 PRINT "3. R = SIN(7*Z)"
250 PRINT
260 PRINT "4. R = 1+2*COS(Z)"
270 PRINT
280 PRINT "5. R = 1+COS(Z)"
290 PRINT
300 PRINT "6. R = 1+SIN(2*Z)"
310 PRINT
320 PRINT "7. R = 1+2*COS(2*Z)"
330 PRINT
340 PRINT "TYPE IN THE NUMBER OF"
350 PRINT "THE EQUATION";
360 INPUT N
370 IF N=1 THEN DEF FNA(Z)=1
380 IF N=2 THEN DEF FNA(Z)=SIN(2*Z)
390 IF N=3 THEN DEF FNA(Z)=SIN(7*Z)
400 IF N=4 THEN DEF FNA(Z)=1+2*COS(Z)
410 IF N=5 THEN DEF FNA(Z)=1+COS(Z)
420 IF N=6 THEN DEF FNA(Z)=1+SIN(2*Z)
430 IF N=7 THEN DEF FNA(Z)=1+2*COS(2*Z)
440 PRINT
450 PRINT "FOR STANDARD PLOT USE A=1 AND B=1"
460 PRINT
470 PRINT "VALUE OF A";
480 INPUT A
490 PRINT
500 PRINT "VALUE OF B";
510 INPUT B
520 PRINT
```

SX and SY denote the number of points that can be plotted on the screen. Put in the values appropriate for your computer. The number RATIO is used to make a circle look like a circle. Try other values if 0.6 does not work.

```
600 REM %%%%%%%%%%%%%%%%%%%%%% CALCULATING RANGE OF R %%%%%%%%%%%%%%%%%%%%%%
610 PRINT "CALCULATING RANGE OF R"
620 LET M=1.0E-30
630 FOR Z=0 TO 2*π STEP 0.1 : REM π=PI
640 LET R=ABS(FNA(Z))
650 IF M<R THEN LET M=R+0.1
660 NEXT Z
670 PRINT "READY FOR PLOTTING"
680 FOR I=1 TO 1000
690 NEXT I
700 PRINT CS$ : REM CLS
710 GOSUB 1010 : REM PREPARE SCREEN IF NECESSARY
800 REM %%%%%%%%%%%%%%%%%%%%%% PLOTTING %%%%%%%%%%%%%%%%%%%%%%%%%%%%%%%%%%%%
810 FOR Z=0 TO 2*π STEP 0.01 : REM π=PI
820 LET R=FNA(Z)
830 LET U=HX+HY*RATIO*COS(A*Z)*R/M
840 IF U<0 OR U>SX THEN GOTO 880
850 LET V=HY+HY*SIN(B*Z)*R/M
860 IF V<0 OR V>SY THEN GOTO 880
870 GOSUB 1110 : REM PLOT U,V
880 NEXT Z
900 REM %%%%%%%%%%%%%%%%%%%%%% ENDING AND ANOTHER GO %%%%%%%%%%%%%%%%%%%%%%
910 GET G$ : REM LET G$=INKEY$
920 IF G$="" THEN GOTO 910
930 GOSUB 1210 : REM RESTORE SCREEN IF NECESSARY
940 PRINT CS$ : REM CLS
950 PRINT " ANOTHER GO?  Y OR N"
960 GET G$ : REM LET G$=INKEY$
970 IF G$<>"Y" AND G$<>"N" THEN GOTO 960
980 IF G$="Y" THEN GOTO 170
990 END : REM STOP
1000 REM %%%%%%%%%%%%%%%%%%%%%% PREPARE HI-RES SCREEN FOR VIC 20 %%%%%%%%%%
1010 POKE 36869,R8+12:POKE 36867,(PEEK(36867) AND 128) OR 25
1020 POKE 36866,R5-4:POKE 36864,R3+4
1030 FOR I=RR TO SS:POKE I,0:NEXT I
1040 FOR I=0 TO 219:POKE PP+I,I-32*Q:POKE QQ+I,2:NEXT I
1050 RETURN
1100 REM %%%%%%%%%%%%%%%%%%%%%% PLOT VIA POKE FOR VIC 20 %%%%%%%%%%%%%%%%%%
1110 V=SY-V
1120 J=INT(U/8)
1130 L=INT(U-8*J)
1140 I=INT(V/16)
1150 K=INT(V-16*I)
1160 W=RR+I*288+J*16+K
1170 POKE W,PEEK(W) OR 2↑(7-L)
1180 RETURN
1200 REM %%%%%%%%%%%%%%%%%%%%%% RESTORE SCREEN FOR VIC 20 %%%%%%%%%%%%%%%%%
1210 POKE 36869,R8:POKE 36867,R6
1220 POKE 36866,R5:POKE 36864,R3:POKE 198,0
1230 RETURN
1300 REM %%%%%%%%%%%%%%%%%%%%%% VIC 20 SETTINGS %%%%%%%%%%%%%%%%%%%%%%%%%%%
1310 Q=PEEK(44)>=18:PP=7680+Q*3584:QQ=38400+Q*512
1320 IFQ=-1ANDPEEK(44)<32 THEN PRINT"PROGRAM ABORTED - SEE APPENDIX":END
1330 RR=4096-Q*512:SS=RR+3583:R8=PEEK(36869):R6=PEEK(36867)
1340 R5=PEEK(36866):R3=PEEK(36864)
1350 RETURN
```

This part calculates the range of R (approximately, to save time). The graph is then scaled to fill your screen.

This PLOTs the graph. A check is made to ensure that only the points that will fit on the screen are plotted. Use PLOT or POKE as appropriate.

Use the appropriate POKEs for your microcomputer.

```
         POLAR GRAPHICS
  1.  R = 1
  2.  R = SIN(2*Z)
  3.  R = SIN(7*Z)
  4.  R = 1+2*COS(Z)
  5.  R = 1+COS(Z)
  6.  R = 1+SIN(2*Z)
  7.  R = 1+2*COS(2*Z)
  TYPE IN THE NUMBER OF
  THE EQUATION? 3
  FOR STANDARD PLOT USE
  A=1 AND B=1
  VALUE OF A? 1
  VALUE OF B? 3
```

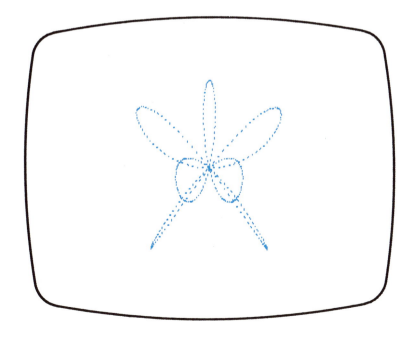

```
10 REM                ******************
20 REM                *    SINCLAIR    *
30 REM                * POLAR GRAPHICS *
40 REM                *                *
50 REM                ******************
60 REM
70 REM
100 REM %%%%%%%%%%%%%%%%%%%%% SETTING UP %%%%%%%%%%%%%%%%%%%%%%%%%%%%
120 LET SX=62
130 LET SY=42
140 LET RATIO=0.6
150 LET HY=SY/2
160 LET HX=SX/2
170 CLS
180 PRINT "   POLAR GRAPHICS"
190 PRINT
200 PRINT "1. R = 1"
210 PRINT
220 PRINT "2. R = SIN(2*Z)"
230 PRINT
240 PRINT "3. R = SIN(7*Z)"
250 PRINT
260 PRINT "4. R = 1+2*COS(Z)"
270 PRINT
280 PRINT "5. R = 1+COS(Z)"
290 PRINT
300 PRINT "6. R = 1+SIN(2*Z)"
310 PRINT
320 PRINT "7. R = 1+2*COS(2*Z)"
330 PRINT
340 PRINT "TYPE IN THE NUMBER OF"
350 PRINT "THE EQUATION ";
360 INPUT N
365 PRINT N
370 IF N=1 THEN LET A$="1"
380 IF N=2 THEN LET A$="SIN(2*Z)"
390 IF N=3 THEN LET A$="SIN(7*Z)"
400 IF N=4 THEN LET A$="1+2*COS(Z)"
410 IF N=5 THEN LET A$="1+COS(Z)"
420 IF N=6 THEN LET A$="1+SIN(2*Z)"
430 IF N=7 THEN LET A$="1+2*COS(2*Z)"
440 PRINT
450 PRINT "FOR STANDARD PLOT USE A=1 AND B=1"
460 PRINT
470 PRINT "VALUE OF A ";
480 INPUT A
485 PRINT A
490 PRINT
500 PRINT "VALUE OF B ";
510 INPUT B
515 PRINT B
520 PRINT
600 REM %%%%%%%%%%%%%%%%%%%% CALCULATING RANGE OF R %%%%%%%%%%%%%%%%%%%%
610 PRINT "CALCULATING RANGE OF R"
620 LET M=1.0E-30
630 FOR Z=0 TO 2*PI STEP 0.1
640 LET R=ABS(VAL(A$))
650 IF M<R THEN LET M=R+0.1
```

SX and SY denote the number of points that can be plotted on the screen. Put in the values appropriate for your computer. The number RATIO is used to make a circle look like a circle. Try other values if 0.6 does not work. For the ZX Spectrum use 0.92.

This part calculates the range of R (approximately, to save time). The graph is then

UP AND DOWN, ROUND AND ROUND

```
660 NEXT Z
670 PRINT "READY FOR PLOTTING"
680 FOR I=1 TO 100
690 NEXT I
700 CLS
800 REM ////////////////////// PLOTTING //////////////////////////
810 FOR Z=0 TO 2*PI STEP 0.01
820 LET R=VAL(A$)
830 LET U=HX+HY*RATIO*COS(A*Z)*R/M
840 IF U<0 OR U>SX THEN GOTO 880
850 LET V=HY+HY*SIN(B*Z)*R/M
860 IF V<0 OR V>SY THEN GOTO 880
870 PLOT U,V
880 NEXT Z
900 REM ////////////////////// ENDING AND ANOTHER GO //////////////////////
910 LET G$=INKEY$
920 IF G$="" THEN GOTO 910
950 PRINT " ANOTHER GO?  Y OR N"
960 LET G$=INKEY$
970 IF G$<>"Y" AND G$<>"N" THEN GOTO 960
980 IF G$="Y" THEN GOTO 170
990 STOP
```

scaled to fill your screen.

This PLOTs the graph. A check is made to ensure that only the points that will fit on the screen are plotted.

See the Appendix for further notes.

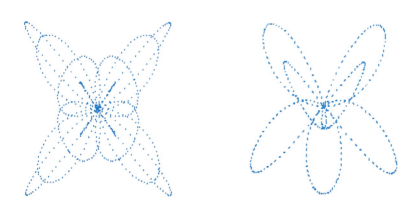

You can be a bit more adventurous and produce some truly marvellous pictures. Instead of using the cartesian coordinates (R*COS(Z),R*SIN(Z)) when plotting, introduce two additional numbers A, B and plot (R*COS(A*Z),R*SIN(B*Z)). By varying A and B you get a spectacular array of beautiful patterns - the choice is limitless. You will find pictures of some of these patterns on the next few pages. Each page uses one equation with the value of A varying from 1 to 9 and the value of B from 1 to 6.

UP AND DOWN, ROUND AND ROUND

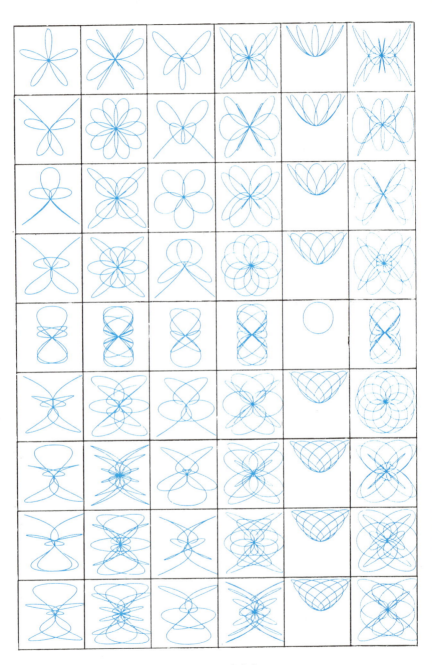

R = SIN(5*Z)

UP AND DOWN, ROUND AND ROUND

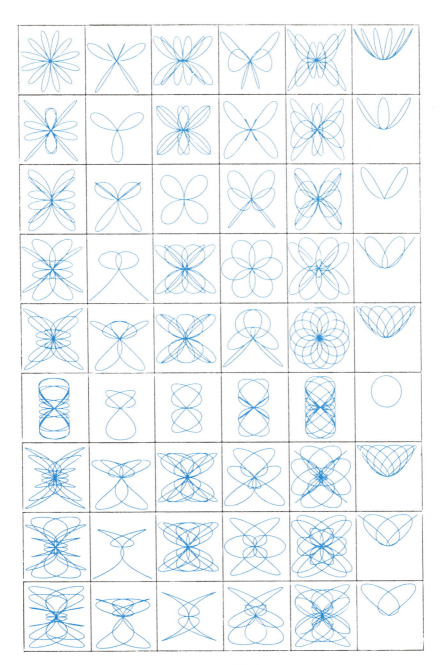

R = SIN(6*Z)

UP AND DOWN, ROUND AND ROUND

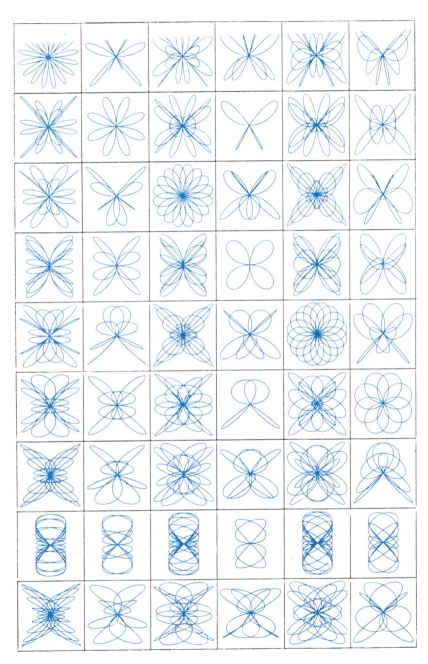

$$R = SIN(8*Z)$$

5 MILES NORTH, 4 MILES EAST
about geometry

Cartesian coordinates tell us how to locate a point in the plane. Below is a map of a treasure island (drawn by one of my daughters). The various places can be located by using coordinates. For example, the buried treasure is at location (2,-2) while the landing stage is at (3,2).

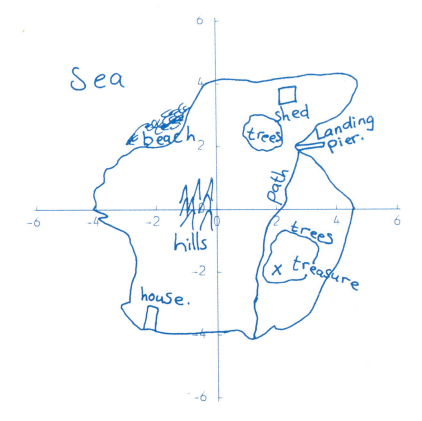

How far away is the treasure from the landing stage? We could walk 1 km East and 4 km South to reach the treasure from the landing stage. This makes a total of 5 km. Of course a shorter path is the straight line path - we will ignore the possibility of hills and other obstacles. This distance (as the crow flies) is SQR(4*4+1*1); about 4.1 km. We have used Pythagoras' theorem to calculate this. Pythagoras was a Greek mathematician and philosopher who was born about 582 BC.

A **right-angled** triangle is a triangle that has a right angle, that is an angle of PI/2 radians or 90 degrees. Pythagoras' theorem states that the square on the longest side (called the hypotenuse) of a right-angled triangle is equal to the sum of the squares on other two sides. If A, B and C denote the lengths of the three sides of a right-angled triangle (with C being the length of the hypotenuse) then $C^2 = A^2 + B^2$.

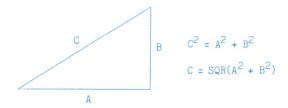

We use Pythagoras' theorem to calculate the (straight line) distance between any two points. Suppose that P is a point with coordinates (XP,YP) and Q is a point with coordinates (XQ,YQ). The distance between P and Q is given by the expression below.

$$SQR((XQ-XP)^2 + (YQ-YP)^2)$$

In words, the distance between P and Q is equal to the square root (SQR) of the sum of the square of the difference in the X-coordinates and the square of the difference in the Y-coordinates.

Let us suppose that you are standing at a point with coordinates (3,4) and a friend is standing at a distance 2 units away. Can you determine the coordinates of your friend? The answer is no, unless you are given more information. In fact the points that are 2 units away from you form a circle of radius 2. To see this let us say that your friend is standing at (X,Y). All we know is that your friend is 2 units away. By using the distance formula we obtain the following equation.

$$SQR((X-3)^2 + (Y-4)^2) = 2$$

This may be rewritten as follows.

$(X-3)^2 + (Y-4)^2 = 4$

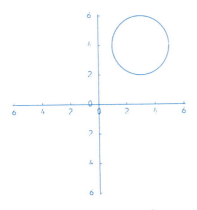

If you plot all the points of the form (X,Y) which satisfy this equation then you get a circle of radius 2. For each value of X you could find which values of Y (if any) satisfy the equation. Notice that X has to be between 1 and 5, otherwise the point (X,Y) will be more than 2 units away from (3,4). If, for example, we let X be 3 then our equation becomes

$(3-3)^2 + (Y-4)^2 = 4$

This simplifies to $(Y-4)^2 = 4$, and so we conclude that $(Y-4) = SQR(4)$ or $(Y-4) = -SQR(4)$. In other words Y = 6 or Y = 2. Thus the two points (3,5) and (3,2) lie on the circle. By choosing different values of X you can find other points on the circle.

More generally, the equation of a circle of radius R and centre (XP,YP) is given by the equation below.

$(X-XP)^2 + (Y-YP)^2 = R^2$

In the computer game TREASURE HUNT, there are a number of bushes neatly displayed on your screen. Some treasure is hidden under one of these bushes. You have to work out where the treasure is hidden. You are located at the bush that is flashing and you can move from bush to bush by pressing one of U, D, R or L. By pressing * you will be told approximately how far away the treasure is from you. In fact if D is the distance between you and the treasure then your microcomputer will display INT(D), the integral part of D. This is just the value of D ignoring the decimal part. Thus if the number displayed is D then you know that the treasure is D or more units away, but less than D+1 units away.

There are two other features to TREASURE HUNT. First, if the distance between you and the treasure is 10 or more then an X is displayed instead of a number. Secondly, the distance is printed only about half of the time. The rest of the time a question mark is printed.

5 MILES NORTH, 4 MILES EAST

Using logic and geometric insight, or just plain guesswork, try and locate the treasure in as few moves as you can. If you are clever and lucky you may be able to find the treasure in about three guesses.

```
10 REM
20 REM                    ******************
30 REM                    *                *
40 REM                    *  TREASURE HUNT *
50 REM                    *                *
60 REM                    ******************
70 REM
100 REM %%%%%%%%%%%%%%%%%%%% SETTING UP %%%%%%%%%%%%%%%%%%%%%%%%%%%%%
110 LET CS$=CHR$(147) : REM CODE FOR CLEAR SCREEN
120 LET HM$=CHR$(19) : REM CODE FOR HOME
130 LET S=ASC("0") : REM LET S=CODE("0")
140 LET P=10 : REM NUMBER OF VERT BUSHES
150 LET Q=9 : REM NUMBER OF HORIZ BUSHES
160 DIM A$(P,Q)
170 FOR I=1 TO P
180 FOR J=1 TO Q
190 LET A$(I,J)="#" : REM LET A$(I,J)="#"
200 NEXT J
210 NEXT I
220 LET M=5
230 LET N=5
240 LET MM=INT(RND(1)*P+1)
250 LET NN=INT(RND(1)*Q+1)
260 PRINT CS$ : REM CLS
270 GOSUB 710
300 REM %%%%%%%%%%%%%%%%%%%% THE LOOP %%%%%%%%%%%%%%%%%%%%%%%%%%%%%%
310 LET B$=A$(M,N)
320 LET A$(M,N)=" "
330 GOSUB 910
340 LET A$(M,N)=B$
350 GOSUB 910
400 REM %%%%%%%%%%%%%%%%%%%% YOUR MOVE %%%%%%%%%%%%%%%%%%%%%%%%%%%%%
410 GET G$ : REM LET G$=INKEY$
420 IF G$="D" AND M<P THEN LET M=M+1
430 IF G$="U" AND M>1 THEN LET M=M-1
440 IF G$="R" AND N<Q THEN LET N=N+1
450 IF G$="L" AND N>1 THEN LET N=N-1
460 IF G$="*" AND A$(M,N)="#" THEN GOTO 510 : REM "※"
470 GOTO 310
500 REM %%%%%%%%%%%%%%%%%%%% PRINT DISTANCE & CHECK FOR END %%%%%%%%%%%%
510 LET DIST=INT(SQR((MM-M)*(MM-M)+(NN-N)*(NN-N)))
520 LET A$(M,N)=CHR$(S+DIST)
530 IF DIST=0 THEN GOTO 610
540 IF DIST>9 THEN LET A$(M,N)="X"
550 IF RND(1)<.5 THEN LET A$(M,N)="?"
560 GOTO 310
```

There are P by Q bushes. In this program P is 10 and Q is 9. Change these values if you want to. The array A$(I,J) stores the relevant information.

The treasure is hidden behind the bush A$(MM,NN).

```
600 REM %%%%%%%%%%%%%%%%%%%%%% ENDING AND ANOTHER GO %%%%%%%%%%%%%%%%%%%%%%
610 GOSUB 710
620 GOSUB 1010 : REM SOUND EFFECTS
630 PRINT " ANOTHER GO? Y OR N";
640 GET G$ : REM LET G$=INKEY$
650 IF G$<>"Y" AND G$<>"N" THEN GOTO 640
660 IF G$="Y" THEN GOTO 170
670 END : REM STOP
700 REM %%%%%%%%%%%%%%%%%%%%%% PRINT DISPLAY %%%%%%%%%%%%%%%%%%%%%%%%
710 PRINT HM$; : REM PRINT AT 0,0
720 PRINT " U=UP  *=LOOK R=RIGHT"
730 PRINT " D=DOWN        L=LEFT"
740 FOR I=1 TO P
750 PRINT " ";
760 FOR J=1 TO Q
770 PRINT " ";A$(I,J);
780 NEXT J
790 PRINT
800 PRINT
810 NEXT I
820 RETURN
900 REM %%%%%%%%%%%%%%%%%%%%%% FLASH BUSH %%%%%%%%%%%%%%%%%%%%%%%%%%%%
905 REM USE  PRINT AT 2*M,2*N;A$(M,N)  IF AVAILABLE
910 PRINT HM$;
920 FOR I=1 TO 2*M
930 PRINT
940 NEXT I
950 PRINT TAB(2*N) A$(M,N)
960 RETURN
1000 REM %%%%%%%%%%%%%%%%%%%%%% SOUND EFFECTS %%%%%%%%%%%%%%%%%%%%%%%%
1010 POKE 36878,15 : K=1
1020 T=250-K*20 : K=K+1
1030 POKE 36876,T
1040 FOR I=1 TO 200 : NEXT
1050 POKE 36876,0
1060 IF K<4 THEN 1020
1070 POKE 36878,0
1080 RETURN
```

If your microcomputer has a PRINT AT facility then use it instead of lines 910-950.

Place your own sound effects here.

See the Appendix for further notes.

5 MILES NORTH, 4 MILES EAST

```
      TREASURE   HUNT
U=UP    *=LOOK  R=RIGHT
D=DOWN          L=LEFT
 ?  9  #  #  #  #  #  #  #

 8  #  #  #  #  #  #  #  #

 #  #  #  #  #  #  #  #  #

 #  #  #  #  #  #  #  #  #

 #  #  #  #  5  #  #  #  #

 #  #  #  #  #  #  #  #  #

 #  ?  #  #  #  #  #  #  #

 2  #  2  #  #  #  #  #  #

 ?  1  #  #  3  #  #  #  #

 #  #  #  #  #  #  #  #  #
```

```
      TREASURE   HUNT
U=UP    *=LOOK  R=RIGHT
D=DOWN          L=LEFT
 X  X  #  #  ?  ?  ?  #  ?

 X  ?  #  #  #  #  #  #  ?

 #  ?  #  #  #  #  #  #  #

 #  #  #  #  #  #  #  #  #

 #  #  #  #  5  #  #  #  #

 #  #  #  5  #  #  #  #  #

 #  #  #  #  #  #  #  #  3

 #  #  #  #  #  #  2  ?  ?

 7  #  #  #  #  #  ?  ?  #

 7  #  #  #  #  #  ?  #  1
```

STRETCHING AND SHRINKING

about matrices

Drawing pictures with your computer is fun. Sometimes, after you have produced a picture you want to change it by stretching or shrinking it in some direction. You can do this quite easily with **matrices.**

Suppose that the picture we are interested in is the one shown below.

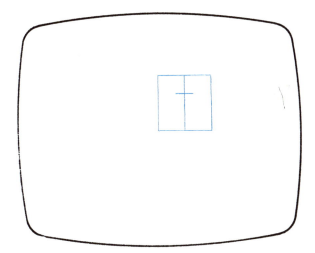

You can obtain such a picture on your screen by PLOTting or POKEing the appropriate points. The program MATRIX INVESTIGATION, which appears later on, will do this for you.

It helps to put some coordinate axes around our picture. The result is shown overleaf.

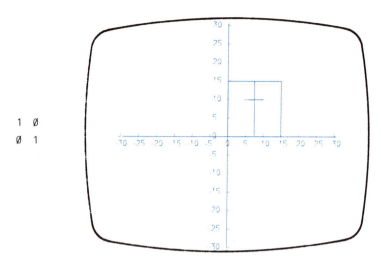

What would you do if you wanted to stretch the picture horizontally so that it became twice its present width? Simply doubling the value of the horizontal or X coordinates will produce the desired effect. Thus, if originally we plotted a point with coordinates (X,Y), we now plot it with coordinates (2*X,Y). For example, we originally plotted a point at (15,15), now we plot that point at (30,15).

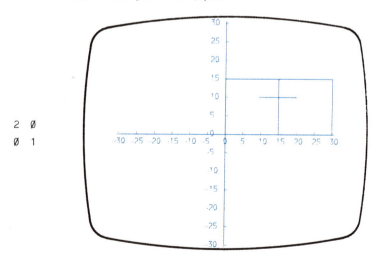

You may want to do something a bit more fancy. For example, make the picture lean over the right. You can achieve this by plotting the points

(X+Y,Y) instead of (X,Y). For example, in the original picture we plotted a point with coordinates (0,15), now we plot (15,15).

1 1
0 1

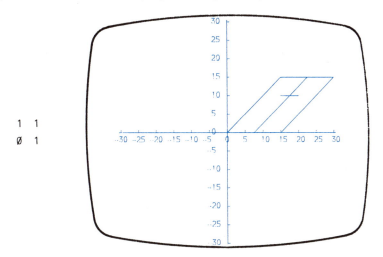

We can be even more adventurous. Instead of plotting (X,Y), let us plot (X+Y,Y+X/3). For example, in the original picture we plotted a point at (15,15), we now plot a point at (30,20) instead. The resulting picture is shown below.

1 1
1/3 1

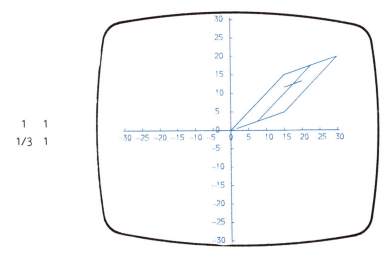

More generally we can plot (M1*X+M2*Y,M3*X+M4*Y), instead of (X,Y), where M1, M2, M3, M4 are any numbers that you care to choose. For each different choice you get a different looking picture. The numbers M1, M2, M3, M4 are usually stored in a square arrangement.

```
M1  M2
M3  M4
```

Such a square arrangement is called a **matrix,** which is another name for a two-dimensional array of numbers M(I,J) where

```
M(1,1) = M1    M(1,2) = M2
M(2,1) = M3    M(2,2) = M4
```

The matrix corresponding to each of the pictures shown appears on the left side of each picture.

Note that the matrix

```
1  ∅
∅  1
```

does nothing to a picture - it is called the **identity** matrix.

Another example showing the effect of a matrix on our picture is given below.

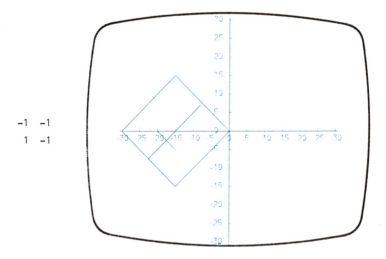

An important number associated with matrices is the number

M1*M4 - M2*M3

which is called the **determinant** of the matrix. Its value tells us how much

STRETCHING AND SHRINKING

stretching or shrinking occurs. Shrinking usually occurs when the determinant is between -1 and 1, otherwise stretching takes place. If the determinant is 0 then strange things happen. The picture gets squashed onto a line and becomes unrecognisable. This will happen, for example, with the matrix given below. The result is also shown below.

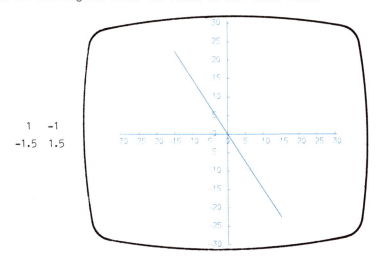

```
  1    -1
-1.5   1.5
```

You can investigate the effect that a matrix has on a picture with the program MATRIX INVESTIGATION. On RUNning the program you will be asked to INPUT the matrix term by term. The determinant of the matrix will be displayed. You will then have the opportunity to change the matrix before the new picture is drawn.

```
10 REM                  **************************
20 REM                  *                        *
30 REM                  * MATRIX INVESTIGATION *
40 REM                  *                        *
50 REM                  **************************
60 REM
70 REM
100 REM %%%%%%%%%%%%%%%%%%%%% SETTING UP %%%%%%%%%%%%%%%%%%%%%%%%%%%%%%
110 LET CS$=CHR$(147) : REM CODE FOR CLEAR SCREEN
120 LET SX=176 : REM SCREEN SIZE HORIZ
130 LET SY=160 : REM SCREEN SIZE VERT
140 LET RATIO=0.6 : REM TO MAKE HORIZ & VERT LINES SAME LENGTH
150 LET HX=SX/2
160 LET HY=SY/2
165 GOSUB 1310 : REM EXTRA SETTINGS FOR VIC 20
170 REM %%%%%%%%% MATRIX INPUT %%%%%%%%%%%%%
180 PRINT CS$ : REM CLS
190 PRINT " MATRIX INVESTIGATION"
200 PRINT
```

Use values of SX, SY and RATIO to suit your computer.

```
210 PRINT "TYPE IN YOUR MATRIX"
220 PRINT
230 PRINT "ROW 1 COLUMN 1 ";
240 INPUT M1
250 PRINT "ROW 1 COLUMN 2 ";
260 INPUT M2
270 PRINT
280 PRINT "ROW 2 COLUMN 1 ";
290 INPUT M3
300 PRINT "ROW 2 COLUMN 2 ";
310 INPUT M4
320 PRINT
330 PRINT "YOUR MATRIX IS:"
340 PRINT TAB(4);M1;TAB(10);M2
350 PRINT TAB(4);M3;TAB(10);M4
360 PRINT
370 LET DET=M1*M4-M2*M3
380 PRINT "DETERMINANT IS ";DET
390 PRINT
400 PRINT "DO YOU WISH TO CARRY"
410 PRINT "ON? Y OR N"
420 PRINT
430 GET G$ : REM LET G$=INKEY$
440 IF G$<>"Y" AND G$<>"N" THEN GOTO 430
450 IF G$="N" THEN GOTO 180
460 PRINT " OK   HERE WE GO"
470 PRINT " PLEASE BE PATIENT "
480 FOR I=1 TO 1000
490 NEXT I
500 LET DD=ABS(DET)
510 IF DD<1 THEN LET DD=1
520 PRINT CS$ : REM CLS
530 GOSUB 1010 : REM PREPARE SCREEN IF NECESSARY
600 REM %%%%%%%%%%%%%%%%%%%%%%% THE PICTURE %%%%%%%%%%%%%%%%%%%%%%%%%%%
610 FOR X=0 TO 15 STEP 7.5
620 FOR Y=0 TO 15 STEP 1/DD
630 GOSUB 910
640 NEXT Y
650 NEXT X
660 FOR Y=0 TO 15 STEP 15
670 FOR X=0 TO 15 STEP 1/DD
680 GOSUB 910
690 NEXT X
700 NEXT Y
710 LET Y=12
720 FOR X=5 TO 10 STEP 1/DD
730 GOSUB 910
740 NEXT X
800 REM %%%%%%%%%%%%%%%%%%%%%% ENDING AND ANOTHER GO %%%%%%%%%%%%%%%%%%%%%
810 GOSUB 1210 : REM RESTORE SCREEN IF NECESSARY
820 PRINT CS$ : REM CLS
830 PRINT " ANOTHER GO?  Y OR N"
840 GET G$ : REM LET G$=INKEY$
850 IF G$<>"Y" AND G$<>"N" THEN GOTO 840
860 IF G$="Y" THEN GOTO 180
870 END : REM STOP
```

This part INPUTs the matrix.

The matrix is   M1 M2
                 M3 M4

See the Appendix for further notes. See also the notes with the GRAPH PLOTTING programs.

Create your own picture if you prefer.

STRETCHING AND SHRINKING

```
900 REM %%%%%%%%%%%%%%%%%%%% DRAWING %%%%%%%%%%%%%%%%%%%%%%%%%%%%%
910 LET U=(M1*X+M2*Y)*RATIO+HX
920 IF U<0 OR U>SX THEN RETURN
930 LET V=HY+M3*X+M4*Y
940 IF V<0 OR V>SY THEN RETURN
950 GOSUB 1110 : REM PLOT U,V
960 RETURN
1000 REM %%%%%%%%%%%%%%%%%%%% PREPARE HI-RES SCREEN FOR VIC 20 %%%%%%%%%
1010 POKE 36869,R8+12:POKE 36867,(PEEK(36867) AND 128) OR 21
1020 FOR I=RR TO SS:POKE I,0:NEXT I
1030 FOR I=0 TO 219:POKE PP+I,I-32*Q:POKE QQ+I,2:NEXT I
1040 RETURN
1100 REM %%%%%%%%%%%%%%%%%%%% POKE POSITIONS FOR VIC 20 %%%%%%%%%%%%%%%%%
1110 V=SY-V
1120 J=INT(U/8)
1130 L=INT(U-8*J)
1140 I=INT(V/16)
1150 K=INT(V-16*I)
1160 W=RR+I*352+J*16+K
1170 POKE W,PEEK(W) OR 2↑(7-L)
1180 RETURN
1200 REM %%%%%%%%%%%%%%%%%%%% RESTORE SCREEN FOR VIC 20 %%%%%%%%%%%%%%%%%
1210 POKE 198,0
1220 GET G$:IF G$="" THEN 1220
1230 POKE 36869,R8:POKE 36867,R6:POKE 198,0
1240 RETURN
1300 REM %%%%%%%%%%%%%%%%%%%% VIC 20 SETTINGS %%%%%%%%%%%%%%%%%%%%%%%%%%%
1310 Q=PEEK(44)>=18:PP=7680+Q*3584:QQ=38400+Q*512
1320 IFQ=-1ANDPEEK(44)<32THEN PRINT."PROGRAM ABORTED - SEE APPENDIX":END
1330 RR=4096-Q*512:SS=RR+3583:R8=PEEK(36869):R6=PEEK(36867)
1340 RETURN
```

Notice the terms M1*X+M2*Y and M3*X+M4*Y.

Use the appropriate POKEs for your microcomputer if PLOT is not available.

```
        MATRIX INVESTIGATION

    TYPE IN YOUR MATRIX

    ROW 1 COLUMN 1 ? 1
    ROW 1 COLUMN 2 ? 1

    ROW 2 COLUMN 1 ? .333
    ROW 2 COLUMN 2 ? 1

    YOUR MATRIX IS:
           1     1
           .333  1

    DETERMINANT IS   .667

    DO YOU WISH TO CARRY
    ON? Y OR N

      OK  HERE WE GO
      PLEASE BE PATIENT
```

Matrices are very important in mathematics. They are not just used for stretching and shrinking pictures; for instance matrices are used in solving simultaneous linear equations.

The matrices that we have looked at so far are two-by-two matrices; they have two rows and two columns. Matrices in general can be of any size, and they do not have to be square. Any rectangular array of numbers is called a **matrix.** As an example, the following is a four-by-six matrix with four rows and six columns.

1	3	-2	1	9	-1
0	2	1	-6	7	0
9	2	0	0.5	4	1.2
7	6.3	0	5	7.9	9

A matrix is a useful shorthand device for storing information. The next chapter shows some further applications of matrices.

PLAYING THE GAME
about games of strategy

There are, roughly speaking, three sorts of games: games of chance, games of skill and games of strategy. The games of chance include games such as roulette, bingo, etc. To play such games essentially involves little skill; good luck is what you need, although an understanding of probability may help you to see why you are losing. The games of skill include games such as golf, cricket, hockey, etc. In these games it is clear what you have to do; the problem is in actually doing it - practice helps. Also included here are puzzles such as Rubik's cube; mathematics can help solve such games - see the next chapter. The third variety of games, games of stategy, include noughts and crosses (tic-tac-toe), chess, monopoly, draughts, paper-stone-scissors, etc. Here you and your opponent, or opponents, are presented with a number of possible choices. You then have to make a decision. For example, strategy plays an important role in chess; luck alone will not win the game for you. This chapter is about **games of strategy.**

Many games of strategy were originally conceived as training aids for certain aspects of life. For example, it is clear that chess has military origins while monopoly has capitalist origins. In real life, whenever two or more individuals make decisions that involve conflicting interests then we have a competitive situation. Many such situations arise in the economic, social, political and military world. A branch of mathematics known as **game theory** is useful in handling such competitive situations. It is an attempt to provide the competitors with a process whereby they can optimise (maximise) their gains. Real life situations may be studied by game theory but there is a danger that people just become numbers and losing a few in a battle is just part of the game.

For simplicity we shall only look at games of strategy involving two players. Possibly one of the players is "nature" Each player may be an individual, a leader of an army or union, or even an army or union itself. In addition we shall assume that what one player gains the other one loses. Thus if one player wins £5 then the other one loses £5. Such a game is called a **two-person zero-sum game**.

The following are four simple examples of two-person zero-sum games.

1. Card matching. Ann has two cards, one black and one white with the number 1 appearing on each. Bill also has two cards, one black with a 1 and one white with a $\emptyset$ on it. The colours and numbers appear on one side so that it is possible to conceal what appears on each card. Ann and Bill simultaneously expose one of their cards. If the colours match then Ann wins (in pounds sterling) the difference between the numbers showing. On the other hand if the cards are different in colour then Bill wins the difference.

2. Matching pennies. Clare and Derek each put down a penny, head or tail up, without showing it to each other. The pennies are uncovered and Clare receives both pennies if they show the same side, otherwise Derek receives them.

3. Two-finger morra. Edward and Fiona each show one or two fingers. If the total number of fingers showing is 2 or 4 then Edward wins that amount in dollars from Fiona. If the total amount is 3 then Fiona wins that amount from Edward.

4. Silver dollars. Kora conceals in her hand 1,2,3 or 4 silver dollars and Inga guesses "even" or "odd". If Inga's guess is correct then she wins the amount that Kora is holding; otherwise Inga must pay Kora the amount that Kora is holding.

Try playing each of these games with a friend.

To help understand such games the first step is to construct a **payoff matrix** (a matrix is a two-dimensional array). To do this, first list all possible choices for each player. For example, in the card matching game Ann has two choices: to either play the black or the white card. These choices are denoted by AB and AW respectively. Similiarly Bill has two choices which we denote by BB and BW. Next write Ann's choices vertically and Bill's horizontally as shown on the top of the next page.

```
     BB BW
AB
AW
```

The next step is to write down how much Ann will win depending on which choice she and Bill make. If Ann chooses AB and Bill chooses BB then Ann wins ∅ (1 - 1 = ∅). We therefore write ∅ in the position which lies in the row containing AB and in the column containing BB. The other positions are similarly filled in, a negative sign being used if Ann loses. The result is called the **payoff matrix** and shows the expected gains of Ann. It equally shows Bill's expected losses; in fact Bill's gains are the negatives of the entries in the payoff matrix.

```
     BB  BW
AB   ∅   -1
AW   ∅    1       payoff to A
```

This payoff matrix may be recorded in an array $A(I,J)$, where $I=1$ TO 2 and $J=1$ TO 2. Thus

$$A(1,1) = ∅, \quad A(1,2) = -1, \quad A(2,1) = ∅, \quad A(2,2) = 1$$

The payoff matrices for the other examples are given below.

```
Card matching         DH  DT
                 CH   2   -2
                 CT  -2    2        payoff to C

Two-finger morra      F1  F2
                 E1   2   -3
                 E2  -3    4        payoff to E

Silver dollars        K1  K2  K3  K4
                 IE  -1   2   -3   4
                 IO   1  -2    3  -4   payoff to I
```

How should the players play? Let us look at the first example - the game of card matching between Ann and Bill. If Ann plays the black card then she either wins ∅ or loses 1. On the other hand if she plays the white card then she either wins ∅ or 1. Surely, therefore, Ann would never play the black card because playing the white card is always better, no matter what Bill does. Thus Ann should always play the white card. Now if Bill plays the black card then he neither loses nor wins anything. However if he plays the white card he could lose 1 (he could only win 1 if Ann plays black, but he can see that she will never do that). Thus Bill should always play the black card. In conclusion Ann would choose AW and Bill would choose BB. The outcome will be that neither player wins or loses anything. Neither player should deviate from this play because to do so could result in a loss.

This game is an example of a **strictly determined** game. Each player has essentially only one choice. Consequently such games get boring very quickly. You can spot a strictly determined game easily because it has the property that there is a number in the payoff matrix which is simultaneously the minimum of a row and the maximum of a column. This number is called a **minimax** point of the payoff matrix.

```
        BB  BW
    AB  0   -1
    AW  0    1
        ↑
      minimax point
```

If the payoff matrix of a game has a minimax point then the game is strictly determined and the players should play the row and column that contains the minimax point. The number in the minimax point is called the **value** of the game; it is the amount that the player playing the rows expects to win on average. In the example above the value of the game is 0 in which case we say that the game is **fair**.

Strictly determined games are not interesting to play (unless your opponent does not notice). Most games are not strictly determined; the three remaining examples given above are not - check this yourself by looking for a minimax point.

In these three examples the situation is much more complicated. The best choice for each player is not so obvious. However if the players play the game a number of times then it is obvious that neither player should make the same choice every time. For example, in the game of matching pennies, if Clare always chooses heads (CH) then Derek would soon spot this and play tails, etc. In fact the best strategy for both Clare and Derek is to play heads and tails randomly. They could do this simply by tossing a coin. The result, over a long period of time, would be a fair game.

PLAYING THE GAME   69

The situation for the two-finger morra game is quite similar. To play optimally Edward and Fiona should make their choices randomly, but with a bias towards holding up one finger. Indeed it can be shown that Edward should choose one finger seven-twelfths of the time and two fingers during the remaining games (five-twelfths of the time). In each case the number of fingers being shown should be chosen randomly. This is Edward's best strategy - or **optimal strategy**. In practise Edward could play his optimal strategy by taking the top card of twelve shuffled cards, seven of which are numbered 1 and the remainder numbered 2. Alternatively Edward could use his computer to choose a random number between 0 and 1. Now if this number is less than 7/12 then Edward should play E1 and hold up one finger, otherwise he should hold up two fingers.

The optimal strategy for Fiona is similar, she should choose one finger seven-twelfths of the time and two fingers five-twelfths of the time.

It is no good deviating from these optimal strategies. By playing their optimal strategies the players minimise the amount they lose.

This game is not fair because if both players play their optimal strategies then on average Edward would lose $1/12 per game. We say that the **value of the game** is -1/12.

Why is the value of this game -1/12? The way to see this is to imagine that Edward and Fiona play the two-finger morra game a large number of times - say 1440 times. We are assuming that each player plays optimally and so on average we would expect Edward to choose one finger (approximately) 840 times (since 1440*7/12 = 840) and two fingers 600 times (since 1440*5/12 = 600). During the 840 times that Edward chooses one we expect Fiona to choose one seven-twelfths of the time, that is 490 times, and two five-twelfths of the time, that is 350 times. Similarly, during the 600 times that Edward chooses two, we expect Fiona to choose one 350 times (since 600*7/12 = 350) and two 250 times (since 600*5/12 = 250). Thus the amount that Edward expects to win during the 1440 games is

$$490*2 + 350*(-3) + 350*(-3) + 250*4 = -120$$

Thus on average he expects to get -120/1440 which is -1/12.

You may like to go through the above calculations assuming that Edward chooses one and two in a proportion different to 5/12 and 7/12. You will find that Edward's expectations will be worse.

PLAYING THE GAME

A **strategy** for a player is just a list of numbers, all non-negative, whose sum is equal to 1. There is one number for each of the possible choices that a player can make; this number gives the proportion of times that that choice should be made. For example, (0.33,0.67) would mean make the first choice 0.33 or 33% of the time and the second 0.67 or 67% of the time. A strategy is an **optimal strategy** if by playing such strategies the players minimise their average losses.

"Solving" a game means finding the optimal strategies for each player and finding the value of the game. There are several techniques for solving two-person zero-sum games. If the size of the payoff matrix is small then there are graphical methods. More generally the method of **linear programming** (the **simplex** method) gives solutions readily. It is beyond our scope to give details of this method; however the program TWO-PERSON ZERO-SUM GAMES is included and uses the simplex method to solve such games. Note that the program does not check whether or not a game is strictly determined - you should be able to do this easily yourself. Note also that often there is more than one optimal strategy for a player - the program only calculates one. You can often find other optimal strategies by writing the players' choices in a different order.

```
10 REM         *******************************
20 REM         *                             *
30 REM         *  TWO-PERSON ZERO-SUM GAMES  *
40 REM         *                             *
50 REM         *******************************
60 REM
70 REM
100 REM //////////////////// SETTING UP ////////////////////////////////
110 LET CS$=CHR$(147) : REM CODE FOR CLEAR SCREEN
120 PRINT CS$; : REM CLS
130 PRINT "TWO-PERSON MATRIX GAME"
140 PRINT "WHAT SIZE IS THE GAME?"
150 PRINT "NUMBER OF ROWS ";
160 INPUT M
170 LET M=INT(M+.5)
180 PRINT "    OF COLUMNS ";
190 INPUT N
200 LET N=INT(N+.5)
210 IF M<2 OR N<2 THEN GOTO 120
220 LET T=M+N+1
230 DIM A(M+1,T+1)
240 DIM P(M)
250 DIM Q(N)
260 LET MIN=0
270 PRINT
280 PRINT "TYPE IN PAYOFF MATRIX"
```

This part INPUTs the payoff matrix for the game to be solved. A typical display is given later on. While the matrix is being INPUT the minimum negative value is calculated and then 1 is subtracted to give MIN.

PLAYING THE GAME

```
290 PRINT
300 FOR I=1 TO M
310 FOR J=1 TO N
320 PRINT "ROW";I;"COLUMN";J;
330 INPUT A(I,J)
340 IF A(I,J)<MIN THEN LET MIN=A(I,J)
350 NEXT J
360 PRINT
370 NEXT I
380 LET MIN=MIN-1
400 REM %%%%%%%%%%%%%%%%%%%%% DISPLAY ARRAY AND SUBTRACT MIN %%%%%%%%%%%%%
410 PRINT C$; : REM CLS
420 FOR I=1 TO M
430 PRINT "   ";
440 FOR J=1 TO N
450 PRINT A(I,J);
460 LET A(I,J)=A(I,J)-MIN
470 NEXT J
480 PRINT
490 NEXT I
495 PRINT
500 REM %%%%%%%%%%%%%%%%%%%%%%% ENLARGING ARRAY %%%%%%%%%%%%%%%%%%%%%%%%%%
510 FOR I=1 TO M+1
520 FOR J=N+1 TO M+N
530 LET A(I,J)=0
540 NEXT J
550 NEXT I
560 FOR J=1 TO N
570 LET A(M+1,J)=-1
580 NEXT J
590 FOR I=1 TO M
600 LET A(I,N+I)=1
610 LET A(I,T)=1
620 LET A(I,T+1)=0
630 NEXT I
640 LET A(M+1,T)=0
650 PRINT "WORKING ";
700 REM %%%%%%%%%%%%%%%%%%%%% CALCULATING LOOP %%%%%%%%%%%%%%%%%%%%%%%%%%
710 PRINT "*";
720 REM %%%%%%%% COLUMN CHOICE S %%%%%%%%
730 LET S=1
740 FOR J=2 TO N+M
750 IF A(M+1,J)<A(M+1,S) THEN LET S=J
760 NEXT J
770 REM %%%%%%%% CHECK FOR FINISH %%%%%%%%
780 IF A(M+1,S)>-1.0E-20 THEN GOTO 1110
790 REM %%%%%%%% ROW CHOICE R %%%%%%%%%%%%
800 LET R=0
810 LET R=R+1
820 IF A(R,S)<1.0E-20 THEN GOTO 810
830 FOR I=R+1 TO M
840 LET C=A(R,N+M+1)/A(R,S)
850 IF A(I,S)<1.0E-20 THEN GOTO 870
860 IF A(I,T)/A(I,S)<C THEN LET R=I
870 NEXT I
```

The payoff matrix is displayed and the value MIN is subtracted from each member of the matrix. The result is that each number in the array is positive.

For calculation purposes the array A(I,J) is enlarged.

This is the main calculating loop. A choice of row R and column S is made according to certain rules. These choices are used to alter the array A(I,J). The process is continued until the array satisfies a certain condition. Each time the program goes through this loop * is printed on the screen.

```
880 REM %%%%%%%% REDUCTION %%%%%%%%%%%%%%%%%%
890 LET A(R,T+1)=S
900 IF S>N THEN LET A(R,T+1)=0
910 LET W=A(R,S)
920 FOR J=1 TO T
930 LET A(R,J)=A(R,J)/W
940 NEXT J
950 FOR I=1 TO M+1
960 IF I=R THEN GOTO 1020
970 LET W=A(I,S)
980 IF ABS(W)<1.0E-20 THEN GOTO 1020
990 FOR J=1 TO T
1000 LET A(I,J)=A(I,J)-A(R,J)*W
1010 NEXT J
1020 NEXT I
1030 GOTO 710
1100 REM %%%%%%%%%%%%%%%%%%%% THE OPTIMAL STRATEGIES %%%%%%%%%%%%%%%%%%%%
1110 LET V=1/A(M+1,N+M+1)
1120 REM %%%%%%%% ROW PLAYER %%%%%%%%%%%%%%
1130 FOR I=1 TO M
1140 LET P(I)=A(M+1,N+I)*V
1150 NEXT I
1160 REM %%%%%%%% COLUMN PLAYER %%%%%%%%%%%
1170 FOR J=1 TO M
1180 LET Q(A(J,T+1))=A(J,T)*V
1190 NEXT J
1200 REM %%%%%%%%%%%%%%%%%%%%%% ENDING DISPLAY %%%%%%%%%%%%%%%%%%%%%%%%%%
1210 PRINT " DONE"
1220 PRINT
1230 PRINT "OPTIMAL STRATEGIES"
1240 PRINT
1250 PRINT "ROW PLAYER"
1260 FOR I=1 TO M
1270 PRINT "    ";INT(1000*P(I)+.5)/1000
1280 NEXT I
1290 PRINT
1300 PRINT "COLUMN PLAYER"
1310 FOR J=1 TO N
1320 PRINT INT(1000*Q(J)+.5)/1000;
1330 NEXT J
1340 PRINT
1350 PRINT
1360 PRINT "VALUE OF GAME TO ROW"
1370 PRINT "PLAYER = ";INT(1000*(V+MIN)+.5)/1000
1400 REM %%%%%%%%%%%%%%%%%%%%%% ANOTHER GO %%%%%%%%%%%%%%%%%%%%%%%%%%%%%
1410 GET G$ : REM LET G$=INKEY$
1420 IF G$="" THEN GOTO 1410
1430 PRINT
1440 PRINT " ANOTHER GO?  Y OR N"
1450 GET G$ : REM LET G$=INKEY$
1460 IF G$<>"Y" AND G$<>"N" THEN GOTO 1450
1470 IF G$="Y" THEN RUN
```

The optimal strategies are calculated.

The optimal strategies and the value of the game are printed out.

See the Appendix for further notes.

```
TWO-PERSON MATRIX GAME

WHAT SIZE IS THE GAME?

NUMBER OF ROWS? 3
       OF COLUMNS? 3

TYPE IN PAYOFF MATRIX

ROW 1 COLUMN 1 ? .3
ROW 1 COLUMN 2 ? -.7
ROW 1 COLUMN 3 ? .7

ROW 2 COLUMN 1 ? -.3
ROW 2 COLUMN 2 ? .7
ROW 2 COLUMN 3 ? -.3

ROW 3 COLUMN 1 ? .4
ROW 3 COLUMN 2 ? 0
ROW 3 COLUMN 3 ? -.5
```

```
     .3 -.7  .7
    -.3  .7 -.3
     .4   0 -.5

WORKING **** DONE

OPTIMAL STRATEGIES

ROW PLAYER
    .381
    .449
    .169

COLUMN PLAYER
 .415   .347   .237

VALUE OF GAME TO ROW
PLAYER =  .047

  ANOTHER GO?  Y OR N
```

How to make money! Ron and Cath often play the following game based on the payoff matrix shown below. Ron chooses one of the rows and Cath chooses one of the columns. The number that appears in the corresponding row and column of the payoff matrix is the amount that Ron wins from Cath. Thus if Ron chooses the first row and Cath chooses the third column then Ron wins 56.

	(1)	(2)	(3)	(4)	(5)
(1)	-7	16	56	-7	10
(2)	1	8	5	-5	-3
(3)	-5	74	43	-6	36
(4)	-6	25	81	-5	24
(5)	-5	-2	9	1	25

payoff to row player (Ron)

If you were playing this game, would you rather choose the rows or the columns? Many people think that it is better to be the row player. In fact it is much better to be the column player. If you can persuade someone to play this game for money with you as the column player then you could make a lot of money. The reason is that the value of the game is -2. Thus if you play your optimal strategy you should on average win 2, although usually you will win a lot more.

The optimal strategy for the column player is to choose only columns 1 and 4, randomly and equally often. In fact you can see that you should never play columns 2, 3 and 5. For example, you should never play column 2 because column 1 <u>always</u> pays better no matter what your opponent chooses. We say that column 1 **dominates** column 2. Similarly column 1 dominates column 3 and column 4 dominates column 5. By crossing out these three columns we get the following (reduced) payoff matrix.

	(1)	(4)
(1)	-7	-7
(2)	1	-5
(3)	-5	-6
(4)	-6	-5
(5)	-5	1

You should now see why this game is grossly unfair to the row player.

If you do find someone to play this game with, do not tell them that you are just playing columns 1 and 4. You can make things "seem" fairer by using ten cards five of which are numbered 1 and the other five are numbered 4. Do not let your opponent see the numbers on your cards. Shuffle your cards and tell your opponent that the number on the top card will be the column that you will choose. Ask your opponent to choose a row while you turn your top card over. Work out the loss or gain from the payoff matrix. How can you lose?

Games with games of strategy. It is quite easy to use your computer to construct entertaining games using some of the above ideas. The program INVESTMENT GAME is a simple example to start you off. In this game an anonymous donor has left you $1000 on condition that you invest it in three companies called X, Y and Z. You must invest all the money for a period of ten years. Each year you must say how much you want to put in each company. You have a sophisticated computer and a spy in each company. You are therefore able to estimate the profit (or loss) per $1 in each company, according to the state of the market. One of three states can occur and the computer tells you the likelihood of a particular one occurring. The profit or loss per $1 is displayed in a table. An example is given below.

```
          MARKET STATES
         ST 1    ST 2    ST 3
         .222    .413    .365

    X     .4     -.4      .3
    Y    -.2      .1      .1
    Z    -.1      .4     -.3
```

In the situation above the likelihood that the first state ST 1 occurs is 0.222 (that is 22.2%). If state ST 1 occurs then for each $1 in company X you gain $0.40, for each $1 in Y you gain -$0.20 (that is you lose $0.20), while for each $1 in Z you lose $0.10. So, if you invested 300, 300 and 400 respectively in X, Y and Z, and if the market was in state ST 1, then you would gain

$$300*0.4 + 300*(-0.2) + 400*(-0.1) = 20$$

and your investment would become $1020.

At the end of each year you must decide where to invest your money. You need only say how much you want to put in X and Y, the computer will automatically invest the remainder in Z.

You have ten years to make your fortune. Each game has a value of 0.05 or thereabouts. Thus, if you invest your money optimally you should increase your investment by 5% or more each year (on average). By gambling you could make or lose a lot more. Good luck.

```
10 REM                   ********************
20 REM                   *                  *
30 REM                   * INVESTMENT GAME  *
40 REM                   *                  *
50 REM                   ********************
60 REM
70 REM
100 REM %%%%%%%%%%%%%%%%%%%% SETTING UP %%%%%%%%%%%%%%%%%%%%%%%%%%%%
110 LET C$=CHR$(147) : REM CODE FOR CLEAR SCREEN
120 DIM A(4,3,10)
130 FOR K=1 TO 10
140 FOR I=1 TO 4
150 FOR J=1 TO 3
160 READ A(I,J,K)
170 NEXT J
180 NEXT I
190 NEXT K
200 LET W=1000
210 LET YEAR=1
300 REM %%%%%%%%%%%%%%%%%%%% LOOP %%%%%%%%%%%%%%%%%%%%%%%%%%%%%%%%%
310 PRINT C$; : REM CLS
315 PRINT "   INVESTMENT GAME"
320 PRINT "   YEAR";YEAR
330 PRINT
340 PRINT "TOTAL AT START OF YEAR IS ";W
350 PRINT
360 PRINT "       MARKET STATES"
370 PRINT "    ST 1   ST 2   ST 3"
380 LET K=INT(RND(1)*10+1)
390 FOR I=1 TO 4
400 IF I=2 THEN PRINT " X";
410 IF I=3 THEN PRINT " Y";
420 IF I=4 THEN PRINT " Z";
430 FOR J=1 TO 3
440 IF I=1 THEN PRINT TAB(-3+6*J);A(I,J,K);
450 IF I>1 THEN PRINT TAB(-2+6*J);A(I,J,K);
460 NEXT J
470 IF I=1 THEN PRINT
480 PRINT
490 NEXT I
500 PRINT
510 PRINT "HOW MUCH DO YOU WANT"
520 PRINT "IN X";
530 INPUT X
540 LET X=INT(X+.5)
550 IF X<0 OR X>W THEN PRINT "ERROR - TRY AGAIN"
560 IF X<0 OR X>W THEN GOTO 520
570 PRINT "IN Y";
580 INPUT Y
590 LET Y=INT(Y+.5)
```

Ten different payoff matrices are read into memory as arrays $A(I,J,K)$. Included in the arrays is the information for the likelihood that a particular market state occurs.

A number K between 1 and 10 is chosen at random and the corresponding payoff matrix is displayed. The computer asks for the amount to be invested in X and Y. The market state is determined by the random number Q in line 650.

```
600 IF Y<0 OR Y>W-X THEN PRINT "ERROR - TRY AGAIN"
610 IF Y<0 OR Y>W-X THEN GOTO 570
620 LET Z=W-X-Y
630 PRINT "REMAINDER";Z;"IN Z"
640 REM %%%%%%%% MARKET STATE %%%%%%%%%%%%
650 LET Q=RND(1)
660 LET R=3
670 IF Q<A(1,1,K)+A(1,2,K) THEN LET R=2
680 IF Q<A(1,1,K) THEN LET R=1
690 PRINT "MARKET IN STATE";R
700 REM %%%%%%%% PROFIT AND LOSS %%%%%%%%%
710 LET W=W+A(2,R,K)*X+A(3,R,K)*Y+A(4,R,K)*Z
720 LET W=INT(W+.5)
730 PRINT "YOUR INVESTMENT IS NOW";W
740 PRINT
750 PRINT "  PRESS Y TO GO ON"
760 GET G$ : REM LET G$=INKEY$
770 IF G$<>"Y" THEN GOTO 760
780 LET YEAR=YEAR+1
790 IF YEAR<11 THEN GOTO 310
800 REM %%%%%%%%%%%%%%%%% ENDING AND ANOTHER GO %%%%%%%%%%%%%%%%%%%%
810 PRINT
820 PRINT "YOU STARTED WITH 1000 AND ENDED WITH";W
830 PRINT
840 LET B$="* A FANTASTIC RESULT *"
850 IF W<2500 THEN LET B$="      * WELL DONE *"
860 IF W<2000 THEN LET B$="    * A GOOD RESULT *"
870 IF W<1750 THEN LET B$="       * NOT BAD *"
880 IF W<1400 THEN LET B$="    * YOU'LL SURVIVE *"
890 IF W<1000 THEN LET B$="BETTER LUCK NEXT TIME"
900 PRINT B$
910 PRINT
1000 REM %%%%%%%% ANOTHER GO %%%%%%%%%%%%
1010 PRINT " ANOTHER GO?  Y OR N"
1020 GET G$ : REM LET G$=INKEY$
1030 IF G$<>"Y" AND G$<>"N" THEN GOTO 1020
1040 IF G$="Y" THEN GOTO 200
1050 END : REM STOP
1100 REM %%%%%%%%%%%%%%%%%% DATA %%%%%%%%%%%%%%%%%%%%%%%%%%%%%%%%%
1110 DATA .478,.337,.185,.3,-.7,.7,-.3,.7,-.3,.2,.1,.5
1120 DATA .106,.53,.364,-.5,-.3,.7,.5,-.5,.7,.3,.5,-.7
1130 DATA .415,.347,.237,.3,-.7,.7,-.3,.7,-.3,.4,0,-.5
1140 DATA .274,.346,.38,.5,-.7,.4,-.3,.7,-.3,-.5,.2,.3
1150 DATA .437,.438,.125,.6,-.6,.4,-.6,.8,-.3,-.3,.5,-.3
1160 DATA .304,.435,.261,.8,-.7,.4,-.6,.4,.2,-.2,.6,-.6
1170 DATA .422,.39,.188,-.5,.8,-.3,.7,-.5,-.3,-.3,.1,.7
1180 DATA .214,.357,.429,.3,-.2,.1,-.3,.4,-.1,.1,-.2,.2
1190 DATA .222,.413,.365,.4,-.4,.3,-.2,.1,.1,-.1,.4,-.3
1200 DATA .093,.463,.444,0,-.6,.7,-.6,0,.2,.2,.8,-.8
```

Line 760 note: This calculates the profit or loss of the investment.

Line 900 note: B$ is the computer's opinion of how well you invested your money.

See the Appendix for further notes.

```
        INVESTMENT GAME

       YEAR 5

  TOTAL AT START OF YEAR
    IS  1854

          MARKET STATES
          ST 1   ST 2   ST 3
          .222   .413   .365

     X    .4    -.4    .3
     Y   -.2    .1     .1
     Z   -.1    .4    -.3

  HOW MUCH DO YOU WANT
  IN X? 1854
  IN Y? 0
  REMAINDER 0 IN Z
  MARKET IN STATE 3
  YOUR INVESTMENT IS NOW
   2410
```

```
          MARKET STATES
          ST 1   ST 2   ST 3
          .274   .346   .38

     X    .5    -.7    .4
     Y   -.3    .7    -.3
     Z   -.5    .2     .3

  HOW MUCH DO YOU WANT
  IN X? 0
  IN Y? 133
  REMAINDER 0 IN Z
  MARKET IN STATE 2
  YOUR INVESTMENT IS NOW
   226
      PRESS Y TO GO ON

  YOU STARTED WITH 1000
  AND ENDED WITH 226

  BETTER LUCK NEXT TIME
```

PLAYING THE GAME

Lines 1100-1200 of the program INVESTMENT GAME contain the necessary data for the array A(I,J,K). If your computer has no DATA statements then you will have to set up the array A(I,J,K) by some other means - for the ZX 81 details are given below.

```
10 REM                    ********************
20 REM                    *      ZX 81       *
30 REM                    * INVESTMENT GAME  *
40 REM                    *                  *
50 REM                    ********************
60 REM
70 REM
100 REM %%%%%%%%%%%%%%%%%%%% SETTING UP FOR THE ZX 81 %%%%%%%%%%%%%%%%%%%%
120 DIM A(4,3,10)
130 FOR K=1 TO 10
135 GOSUB 1100+K*10
140 FOR I=1 TO 4
150 FOR J=1 TO 3
160 LET S=12*I+4*J-15
165 LET A(I,J,K)=VAL(A$(S TO S+3))
170 NEXT J
180 NEXT I
190 NEXT K
200 LET W=1000
210 LET YEAR=1
```

Use lines 300-1050 from INVESTMENT GAME.

```
1100 REM %%%%%%%%%%%%%%%%%%%% DATA %%%%%%%%%%%%%%%%%%%%%%%%%%%%%%%%%%%%%%
1110 LET A$=".478.337.1850.30-0.70.70-0.30.70-0.30.200.10-0.5"
1115 RETURN
1120 LET A$=".106.530.364-0.5-0.30.700.50-0.50.700.300.50-0.7"
1125 RETURN
1130 LET A$=".415.347.2370.30-0.70.70-0.30.70-0.30.400000-0.5"
1135 RETURN
1140 LET A$=".274.346.3800.50-0.70.40-0.30.70-0.3-0.50.200.30"
1145 RETURN
1150 LET A$=".437.438.1250.60-0.60.40-0.60.80-0.3-0.30.50-0.3"
1155 RETURN
1160 LET A$=".304.435.2610.80-0.70.40-0.60.400.20-0.20.60-0.6"
1165 RETURN
1170 LET A$=".422.390.188-0.50.80-0.30.70-0.5-0.3-0.30.100.70"
1175 RETURN
1180 LET A$=".214.357.4290.30-0.20.10-0.30.40-0.10.10-0.20.20"
1185 RETURN
1190 LET A$=".222.413.3650.40-0.40.30-0.20.100.10-0.10.40-0.3"
1195 RETURN
1200 LET A$=".093.463.4440000-0.60.70-0.600000.200.200.80-0.8"
1205 RETURN
```

Approximate solutions. There is another method of finding a solution to games of strategy. Imagine that each player records every move made during a series of games. If the players base their decision on the average of the moves made by their opponent then after a large number of moves each player will have found an optimal strategy. In order to calculate the optimal strategies using this method we do not actually play according to the rules of the game. Instead each player announces, in turn, what he or she will play. This decision is based upon the average of all the announcements made by the opponent.

The method is illustrated with the two-finger morra game played by Edward and Fiona. The payoff matrix of this game is given below.

$$\begin{array}{rr} 2 & -3 \\ -3 & 4 \end{array} \qquad \text{(payoff to Edward)}$$

First of all Edward arbitrarily selects a row which he writes down under the payoff matrix. Let us suppose he selects row 1.

$$\begin{array}{rr} 2 & -3 \\ -3 & 4 \\ \hline 2 & -3 \end{array}$$

Fiona looks at this row and chooses a column corresponding to the smallest number in this row. This is column 2 which Fiona writes to the right of the matrix.

$$\begin{array}{rr|r} 2 & -3 & -3 \\ -3 & 4 & 4 \\ \hline 2 & -3 \end{array}$$

Edward now looks at this column and chooses a row corresponding to the largest number in this column. This is row 2. This row is added, term by term, to the previous row chosen and the result written down below it.

$$\begin{array}{rr|r} 2 & -3 & -3 \\ -3 & 4 & 4 \\ \hline 2 & -3 \\ -1 & 1 \end{array}$$

PLAYING THE GAME 81

Fiona looks at this new row and selects the column corresponding to the smallest number in this row. This is column 1. She adds this column, term by term, to the previously chosen column and writes the result next to it.

```
  2  -3  | -3  -1
 -3   4  |  4   1
 ─────
  2  -3
 -1   1
```

This process is repeated several times. If a tie occurs for the choice of a row (or column) it is resolved by making a random choice.

The result on performing the process ten times is shown below. The smallest number in each row and the largest number in each column have been underlined.

```
  2  -3  | -3  -1   1    3    0   -3  -1   1    3    0  | 6/10
 -3   4  |  4   1  -2   -5   -1    3   0  -3   -6   -2  | 4/10
 ─────
  2  -3
 -1   1
 -4   5
 -2   2
  0  -1
  2  -4
 -1   0
 -4   4
 -2   1
  0  -2
 ─────
 6/10 4/10
```

Approximate strategies can be found by dividing the number of underlined numbers in each row or column by 10. Thus Edward's approximate optimal strategy is (0.6,0.4) while Fiona's is (0.6,0.4). A more accurate answer can be obtained by performing the process a larger number of times.

Computers are well suited to such a method and the program APPROXIMATE GAME ANALYSIS is provided. The computer goes through the process described above 100 times. You could increase this number and consequently get an even more accurate answer.

PLAYING THE GAME

While the TWO-PERSON ZERO-SUM GAMES program provides a quick and accurate solution to a matrix game, the mathematics behind it is quite complicated and no doubt the program is just a "black box" to many. On the other hand the mathematics behind APPROXIMATE GAME ANALYSIS is much easier to follow; you lose because you only get an approximate solution.

```
10 REM           *******************************
20 REM           *                             *
30 REM           *   APPROXIMATE GAME ANALYSIS *
40 REM           *                             *
50 REM           *******************************
60 REM
70 REM
100 REM %%%%%%%%%%%%%%%%%%%% SETTING UP %%%%%%%%%%%%%%%%%%%%%%%%%%%%
110 LET C$=CHR$(147) : REM CODE FOR CLEAR SCREEN
120 LET G=100
130 PRINT C$; : REM CLS
140 PRINT "TWO-PERSON MATRIX GAME "
150 PRINT "WHAT SIZE IS THE GAME?"
160 PRINT "NUMBER OF ROWS";
170 INPUT M
180 LET M=INT(M+.5)
190 PRINT "    OF COLUMNS";
200 INPUT N
210 LET N=INT(N+.5)
220 IF M<2 OR N<2 THEN GOTO 130
230 DIM A(M,N)
240 DIM P(M)
250 DIM Q(N)
260 DIM X(M)
270 DIM Y(N)
280 PRINT
290 PRINT "TYPE IN PAYOFF MATRIX "
300 FOR I=1 TO M
310 FOR J=1 TO N
320 PRINT "ROW";I;"COLUMN";J;
330 INPUT A(I,J)
340 NEXT J
350 PRINT
360 NEXT I
400 REM %%%%%%%%%%%%%%%%%%%% DISPLAY ARRAY %%%%%%%%%%%%%%%%%%%%%%%%
410 PRINT C$; : REM CLS
420 FOR I=1 TO M
430 PRINT "   ";
440 FOR J=1 TO N
450 PRINT A(I,J);
460 NEXT J
470 PRINT
480 NEXT I
490 PRINT
500 REM %%%%%%%%%%%%%%%%%%%% THE GAMES %%%%%%%%%%%%%%%%%%%%%%%%%%%%
510 PRINT "WORKING";
520 LET R=INT(M*RND(1)+1)
530 FOR T=0 TO 9
540 FOR U=1 TO (G+1)/10
```

This section INPUTs the payoff matrix. Two extra arrays X(I) and Y(J) are needed. These store the additional rows and columns needed in the process.

This simply displays the payoff matrix.

This section contains the 100 games played by the computer.

```
550 FOR J=1 TO N
560 LET Y(J)=Y(J)+A(R,J)
570 NEXT J
580 GOSUB 1210
590 LET Q(C)=Q(C)+1
600 FOR I=1 TO M
610 LET X(I)=X(I)+A(I,C)
620 NEXT I
630 GOSUB 1110
640 LET P(R)=P(R)+1
650 NEXT U
660 PRINT "*";
670 NEXT T
680 PRINT "DONE"
690 REM %%%%%%%% THE VALUE %%%%%%%%%%%%%%%%%
700 LET V1=INT(Y(C)+.5)/G
710 LET V2=INT(X(R)+.5)/G
800 REM %%%%%%%%%%%%%%%%%%% ENDING DISPLAY %%%%%%%%%%%%%%%%%%%%%%%%%%%%
810 PRINT
820 PRINT "APPROXIMATE OPTIMAL"
830 PRINT "STRATEGIES"
840 PRINT
850 PRINT "FOR ROW PLAYER"
860 FOR I=1 TO M
870 PRINT "   ";P(I)/G
880 NEXT I
890 PRINT
900 PRINT "COLUMN PLAYER"
910 FOR J=1 TO N
920 PRINT Q(J)/G;
930 NEXT J
940 PRINT
950 PRINT
960 PRINT "VALUE OF GAME TO ROW"
970 PRINT "PLAYER IS >=";V1
980 PRINT "        AND <=";V2
1000 REM %%%%%%%%%%%%%%%%%%%%% ANOTHER GO %%%%%%%%%%%%%%%%%%%%%%%%%%%%%
1010 PRINT
1020 PRINT " ANOTHER GO?  Y OR N"
1030 GET G$ : REM LET G$=INKEY$
1040 IF G$<>"Y" AND G$<>"N" THEN GOTO 1030
1050 IF G$="Y" THEN RUN
1060 END : REM STOP
1100 REM %%%%%%%%%%%%%%%%%%%%% SUBROUTINE FOR MAXIMUM AND MINIMUM %%%%%%%
1200 REM %%%%%%%% MAXIMUM %%%%%%%%%%%%%%%%%%%
1210 LET R=1
1220 FOR I=2 TO M
1230 IF X(I)=X(R) AND RND(1)<0.5 THEN LET R=I
1240 IF X(I)>X(R) THEN LET R=I
1250 NEXT I
1260 RETURN
1300 REM %%%%%%%% MINIMUM %%%%%%%%%%%%%%%%%%%
1310 LET C=1
1320 FOR J=2 TO N
1330 IF Y(J)=Y(C) AND RND(1)<0.5 THEN LET C=J
1340 IF Y(J)<Y(C) THEN LET C=J
1350 NEXT J
1360 RETURN
```

The computer first chooses a row at random. The process described in the text is then iterated 100 times.

If you want your computer to play more games, try changing the value of G in line 120 to 1000. The program will then take longer to RUN, but the result should be more accurate.

This prints out the approximate optimal strategies.

These are just simple subroutines to find the maximum (or minimum) value of a collection of numbers. If there are two such numbers then the computer chooses between them, randomly.

```
TWO-PERSON MATRIX GAME

WHAT SIZE IS THE GAME?

NUMBER OF ROWS? 3
     OF COLUMNS? 3

TYPE IN PAYOFF MATRIX

ROW 1 COLUMN 1 ? .3
ROW 1 COLUMN 2 ? -.7
ROW 1 COLUMN 3 ? .7

ROW 2 COLUMN 1 ? -.3
ROW 2 COLUMN 2 ? .7
ROW 2 COLUMN 3 ? -.3

ROW 3 COLUMN 1 ? .4
ROW 3 COLUMN 2 ? 0
ROW 3 COLUMN 3 ? -.5
```

```
    .3  -.7   .7
   -.3   .7  -.3
    .4   0   -.5

WORKING************DONE

APPROXIMATE OPTIMAL
STRATEGIES

FOR ROW PLAYER
     .39
     .44
     .17

COLUMN PLAYER
  .36   .35   .29

VALUE OF GAME TO ROW
PLAYER IS >= .05
        AND <= .07
```

```
        -1   2  -3   4
         1  -2   3  -4

    WORKING************DONE

    APPROXIMATE OPTIMAL
    STRATEGIES

    FOR ROW PLAYER
         .52
         .48

    COLUMN PLAYER
     .04   .05   .53   .38

    VALUE OF GAME TO ROW
    PLAYER IS >=-.18
            AND <= .01
```

Beer drinking games. Finally here is a game for two beer drinkers. After each has been served with a pint of beer they have to decide who will pay for the round. They do this by writing down a positive integer (a whole number bigger than zero). They then compare the numbers. Whoever wrote the larger number pays for the round, <u>unless</u> that number is bigger by only 1. In that case the person who wrote the smaller number pays for the round <u>and</u> the next round as well. If both beer drinkers have chosen the same number then they play again. The game is fair - what are the optimal strategies?

If you try and use one of the programs TWO-PERSON ZERO-SUM GAMES or APPROXIMATE GAME ANALYSIS you will run into a small problem - what is the size of the game? Each player has infinitely many choices!

The payoff matrix of the game is given on the naxt page. The dots mean that the table has not been completed and is to be continued.

	(1)	(2)	(3)	(4)	(5)	(6)	(7)	(8)	.	.	.
(1)	0	-2	1	1	1	1	1	1	.	.	.
(2)	2	0	-2	1	1	1	1	1	.	.	.
(3)	-1	2	0	-2	1	1	1	1	.	.	.
(4)	-1	-1	2	0	-2	1	1	1	.	.	.
(5)	-1	-1	-1	2	0	-2	1	1	.	.	.
(6)	-1	-1	-1	-1	2	0	-2	1	.	.	.
(7)	-1	-1	-1	-1	-1	2	0	-2	.	.	.
(8)	-1	-1	-1	-1	-1	-1	2	0	.	.	.
.	.	.	.	.	.	.	.	.	.	.	.
.	.	.	.	.	.	.	.	.	.	.	.
.	.	.	.	.	.	.	.	.	.	.	.

You could decide that the players may never choose very large numbers - but is that right? Try RUNning TWO-PERSON ZERO-SUM GAMES limiting the choice of each player to small numbers, for example the first 10. Try other numbers as well, say 9, 8, 7, 6 and 5. If you do this you will find that you always get the same optimal strategies for each player. Indeed, it may be hard to believe, but the best thing that each beer drinker can do is to choose one of the numbers from 1 to 5 (perhaps this is just as well after a couple of rounds). The best strategy for each player is to choose the numbers 1 to 5 with the following frequencies.

        1: 6.25%
        2: 31.25%
        3: 25.00%
        4: 31.25%
        5: 6.25%

Next time you are drinking beer with a friend you might like to suggest this method of deciding who pays for a round. Of course, the game is not restricted to beer drinkers.

REARRANGING THINGS

about groups

If you have played with Rubik's cube then you have probably heard of **groups,** and that they play a key rôle in solving the cube and many other puzzles. Groups are an important branch of mathematics and they figure significantly in other branches of mathematics, in physics, in chemistry and in the other sciences. We shall take a brief look at some of the concepts associated with groups.

The process of rearranging things, for example moving the various faces of the cube, is called a **permutation.** This idea can be illustrated by taking four differently marked squares and placing them in a two-by-two arrangement as illustrated below. For ease the squares have been labelled A,B,C and D, although they have been jumbled around.

```
CCC    BBB
CCC    BBB
CCC    BBB

AAA    DDD
AAA    DDD
AAA    DDD
```

A permutation of the squares rearranges their positions. For example, the process which interchanges the top two squares and leaves the bottom two alone is a permutation which we shall call X. The effect of X on the four squares is shown below.

```
CCC    BBB              BBB    CCC
CCC    BBB              BBB    CCC
CCC    BBB     ──X─→    BBB    CCC

AAA    DDD              AAA    DDD
AAA    DDD              AAA    DDD
AAA    DDD              AAA    DDD
```

Another permutation is to move all the squares around in a clockwise direction. Thus the square in the top-left position is moved to the top-right position, the square that was in the top-right position is moved to the bottom-right position and so on. We shall call this permutation T; its effect on the four squares is illustrated below.

```
CCC  BBB              AAA  CCC
CCC  BBB              AAA  CCC
CCC  BBB      T       AAA  CCC
                ──►
AAA  DDD              DDD  BBB
AAA  DDD              DDD  BBB
AAA  DDD              DDD  BBB
```

Such permutations of the four squares can be vividly demonstrated on your computer by using the program FOUR SQUARES. On RUNning the program type E for experiment. You will see the effect that the permutation X or T has on the four squares by typing X or T.

Two or more permutations can be <u>combined</u> simply by performing them one after the other. For example, we could perform X followed by T.

```
CCC  DDD              DDD  CCC              AAA  DDD
CCC  DDD              DDD  CCC              AAA  DDD
CCC  DDD     X        DDD  CCC     T        AAA  DDD
              ──►                   ──►
AAA  BBB              AAA  BBB              BBB  CCC
AAA  BBB              AAA  BBB              BBB  CCC
AAA  BBB              AAA  BBB              BBB  CCC
```

Any combination of permutations is also a permutation. The combination of X followed by T is written as XT.

```
CCC  DDD              AAA  DDD
CCC  DDD              AAA  DDD
CCC  DDD     XT       AAA  DDD
              ──►
AAA  BBB              BBB  CCC
AAA  BBB              BBB  CCC
AAA  BBB              BBB  CCC
```

Notice that T followed by X (that is TX) does not have the same effect on the four squares as XT. In other words XT and TX are different permutations. We write XT ≠ TX which is read as "XT is not equal to TX".

```
CCC   DDD              CCC   AAA
CCC   DDD              CCC   AAA
CCC   DDD              CCC   AAA
              ──────→
AAA   BBB      TX      BBB   DDD
AAA   BBB              BBB   DDD
AAA   BBB              BBB   DDD
```

A permutation may be combined with itself; for example TT. Notice that doing X twice (that is, doing XX) leaves the squares in their original positions. Similarly doing T four times has the same effect as doing nothing at all. Try this with the FOUR SQUARES program.

The permutation that does nothing is called the **identity** permutation and is denoted by I. It may seem strange to say that doing nothing is a permutation and even to have a symbol for it, but it is no stranger than using the symbol Ø to denote zero or nought. Since the permutations XX and TTTT have the same effect as I we write XX = I and TTTT = I. Notice that any combination of I with a permutation is just that permutation itself. For example, XI = X, TIX = TX, etc.

```
CCC   DDD              CCC   DDD
CCC   DDD              CCC   DDD
CCC   DDD              CCC   DDD
              ──────→
AAA   BBB      I       AAA   BBB
AAA   BBB              AAA   BBB
AAA   BBB              AAA   BBB
```

If we start with some arrangement of the four squares and perform a permutation then we get a new arrangement provided the permutation is not the identity. By repeating this permutation often enough we eventually come back to our original arrangement. The least number of times that we have to perform a permutation in order to get the identity permutation is called the **order** of the permutation. Thus X has order 2 and T has order 4. What about the order of the permutation XT? How many times do we have to perform XT to get the identity? Try it - the answer is 3 which at first may surprise you.

If you experiment with the FOUR SQUARES program then you will soon discover that there are quite a number of different permutations of the four squares. How many different permutations can you find? Be careful; you may have a rather complicated looking combination of permutations which may in fact be quite simple. For example, look at the following combination.

  XTXTTTXTTTXTT

Just because this combination <u>looks</u> complicated does not mean that it is. Indeed, this permutation is the same as X - check this yourself with FOUR SQUARES.

Although there are many possible expressions for permutations as combinations of X and T, there are in fact twenty-four <u>different</u> permutations. These are listed below.

I	X	XT	XTT	XTX	XTTX
T	TX	TXT	TXTT	TXTX	TXTTX
TT	TTX	TTXT	TTXTT	TTXTX	TTXTTX
TTT	TTTX	TTTXT	TTTXTT	TTTXTX	TTTXTTX

Of course there are other ways of expressing these permutations. For example we may rewrite TTTXTTX as XTTXT. Check this yourself with the FOUR SQUARES program.

We call this collection of twenty-four permutations **the group of permutations of four objects,** it provides a good example of a **group.**

An important feature that a group has is that for each permutation in the group there is another permutation (called the **inverse**) which undoes its effect. For example, the inverse of X is X itself, while the inverse of T is the permutation that moves the four squares in an anticlockwise direction. (The inverse of T is also TTT.) The inverse of a permutation is usually denoted by a -1 as a superscript to the symbol for the permutation; for example, X^{-1}, T^{-1}, etc.

```
CCC  DDD        DDD  CCC        CCC  DDD
CCC  DDD        DDD  CCC        CCC  DDD
CCC  DDD   X    DDD  CCC   X    CCC  DDD
AAA  BBB        AAA  BBB        AAA  BBB
AAA  BBB        AAA  BBB        AAA  BBB
AAA  BBB        AAA  BBB        AAA  BBB
```

REARRANGING THINGS

```
CCC  DDD        AAA  CCC         CCC  DDD
CCC  DDD        AAA  CCC         CCC  DDD
CCC  DDD        AAA  CCC         CCC  DDD
          ──T─→                          ──TTT─→
AAA  BBB        BBB  DDD         AAA  BBB
AAA  BBB        BBB  DDD         AAA  BBB
AAA  BBB        BBB  DDD         AAA  BBB


CCC  DDD        AAA  DDD         CCC  DDD
CCC  DDD        AAA  DDD         CCC  DDD
CCC  DDD        AAA  DDD         CCC  DDD
          ──XT─→                         ──XTXT─→
AAA  BBB        BBB  CCC         AAA  BBB
AAA  BBB        BBB  CCC         AAA  BBB
AAA  BBB        BBB  CCC         AAA  BBB
```

The inverse of a combination of permutations is easy to write down. For example, to "undo" the effect of the permutation XTT we simply "undo" each permutation in reverse order. Thus

$$(XTT)^{-1} = T^{-1}T^{-1}X^{-1}$$

No matter how complicated a combination of permutations you have, you can always find the inverse by using this procedure.

We have seen that the order in which two permutations are combined can make a difference. For example, XT and TX are different. We say that X and T do not **commute**. We write this as XT ≠ TX which is read as "XT is not equal to TX". If the order in which we combine two permutations is not important then we say that they commute. Because the group of permutations of four objects has permutations which do not commute we say that this group is **not commutative.**

The program FOUR SQUARES also contains a simple puzzle; press P on RUNning the program. The computer will randomly mix up the four squares for you. The object of the puzzle is to get the four squares into their "correct position". The "correct position" means that square A is in the top-left position, square B is in the top-right position, square C is in the lower-right position and square D is in the lower-left postion. You may only use the permutations X and T, but of course any number of times and in any order. It is good practice to think ahead. Try and do it in at most six moves.

Colour is used in the program FOUR SQUARES. If colours are available on your computer then use the appropriate code numbers. If colour is not available then delete mention of RED$, BLUE$, etc. Thus, for example, delete any mention of the colour codes for the ZX 81. In addition, for the ZX 81, replace lines 170 and 180 by the following:

```
170 DIM A$(4,3)
180 DIM C$(4,3)
```

On some microcomputers (such as the Sinclair range) string variables must be a <u>single</u> letter followed by $. If colour is also available (such as for the ZX Spectrum) you will need to abbreviate the names RED$, GREEN$, BLUE$ and YELLOW$. Do not abbreviate them by using the initial capital letters R$, G$, B$ and Y$ since they are used elsewhere in the program; use some other letters. There is an alternative method. For example, for the ZX Spectrum you replace lines 130-220 by the following lines:

```
170 DIM A$(4,5)
180 DIM C$(4,5)
190 LET A$(1)=CHR$(16)+CHR$(2)+"AAA"
200 LET A$(2)=CHR$(16)+CHR$(4)+"BBB"
210 LET A$(3)=CHR$(16)+CHR$(1)+"CCC"
220 LET A$(4)=CHR$(16)+CHR$(6)+"DDD"
```

```
10 REM                  ****************
20 REM                  *              *
30 REM                  * FOUR SQUARES *
40 REM                  *              *
50 REM                  ****************
60 REM
70 REM
100 REM ///////////////////// SETTING UP /////////////////////////////
110 LET CS$=CHR$(147) : REM CODE FOR CLEAR SCREEN
120 LET HM$=CHR$(19)  : REM CODE FOR HOME
130 LET RED$=CHR$(28)
140 LET GREEN$=CHR$(30)
150 LET BLUE$=CHR$(31)
160 LET YELLOW$=CHR$(158)
170 DIM A$(4)
180 DIM C$(4)
190 LET A$(1)=RED$+"AAA"
200 LET A$(2)=GREEN$+"BBB"
210 LET A$(3)=BLUE$+"CCC"
220 LET A$(4)=YELLOW$+"DDD"
230 FOR I=1 TO 4
240 LET C$(I)=A$(I)
250 NEXT I
```

If colours are available on your computer then put in the appropriate code numbers; otherwise delete RED$, BLUE$, etc.

A$(I) contains the display information. C$(I) is used for the puzzle to check if the squares are in the correct position.

REARRANGING THINGS

```
300 REM %%%%%%%%%%%%%%%%%%%%% EXPERIMENT OR PUZZLE %%%%%%%%%%%%%%%%%%%%%
310 PRINT CS$ : REM CLS
320 PRINT "     FOUR SQUARES"
330 PRINT
340 LET T=0
350 PRINT "FOR EXPERIMENT PRESS E"
360 PRINT "  FOR PUZZLE PRESS P"
370 GET G$ : REM LET G$=INKEY$
380 IF G$<>"E" AND G$<>"P" THEN GOTO 370
390 IF G$="E" THEN LET T=1
400 REM %%%%%%%%%%%%%%%%%%%%% INITIAL DISPLAY %%%%%%%%%%%%%%%%%%%%%%%
410 PRINT CS$ : REM CLS
420 PRINT "     FOUR SQUARES"
430 IF T=0 THEN GOSUB 1210
440 GOSUB 1010
450 PRINT
460 PRINT BLUE$
470 PRINT " X EXCHANGES TOP TWO"
480 PRINT
490 PRINT " T ROTATES CLOCKWISE"
500 PRINT
510 PRINT "    PRESS * TO END"
600 REM %%%%%%%%%%%%%%%%%%%%% YOUR MOVE %%%%%%%%%%%%%%%%%%%%%%%%%%%%%
610 GET G$ : REM LET G$=INKEY$
620 IF G$="" THEN GOTO 610
630 IF G$="X" THEN GOSUB 1310
640 IF G$="T" THEN GOSUB 1410
650 IF G$="*" THEN GOTO 820
660 GOSUB 1010
670 IF T=1 THEN GOTO 610
700 REM %%%%%%%%%%%%%%%%%%%%% CHECK FOR CORRECT POSITION OF SQUARES %%%%%
710 LET K=1
720 IF A$(K)<>C$(K) THEN GOTO 610
730 LET K=K+1
740 IF K<5 THEN GOTO 720

800 REM %%%%%%%%%%%%%%%%%%%%% ENDING AND ANOTHER GO %%%%%%%%%%%%%%%%%%%%
810 GOSUB 1610 : REM FOR NOISE EFFECTS
820 FOR I=1 TO 5
830 PRINT
840 NEXT I
850 PRINT BLUE$
860 PRINT "  ANOTHER GO? Y OR N"
870 GET G$ : REM LET G$=INKEY$
880 IF G$<>"Y" AND G$<>"N" THEN GOTO 870
890 IF G$="Y" THEN GOTO 410
900 END : REM STOP
1000 REM %%%%%%%%%%%%%%%%%%%%% DISPLAY %%%%%%%%%%%%%%%%%%%%%%%%%%%%%%%
1010 PRINT HM$ : REM PRINT AT 0,0
1020 PRINT
1030 PRINT
1040 FOR J=1 TO 3
1050 PRINT TAB(7);A$(1);"  ";A$(2)
1060 NEXT J
1070 PRINT
1080 PRINT
1090 FOR J=1 TO 3
```

The value of T determines whether you are running the experiment (T=1) or the puzzle (T=0).

You have to press X, T or *.

When in puzzle mode this checks to see if the squares are in the correct position.

This displays the four squares.

```
1100 PRINT TAB(7);A$(4);" ";A$(3)
1110 NEXT J
1120 RETURN
1200 REM %%%%%%%%%%%%%%%%%%%% MIXING SUBROUTINE %%%%%%%%%%%%%%%%%%%%
1210 FOR K=1 TO 25
1220 ON INT(RND(1)*3+1) GOSUB 1310,1410,1510
1225 REM GOSUB 1310+INT(RND*3)*100
1230 NEXT K
1240 RETURN
```

For the puzzle, 25 random moves are made.

```
1300 REM %%%%%%%%%%%%%%%%%%%% MOVE X - EXCHANGE TOP TWO SQUARES %%%%%%%%
1310 LET B$=A$(1)
1320 LET A$(1)=A$(2)
1330 LET A$(2)=B$
1340 RETURN
```

This is the subroutine for the move X which exchanges the top two squares.

```
1400 REM %%%%%%%%%%%%%%%%%%%% MOVE T - ROTATE ALL CLOCKWISE %%%%%%%%%%%%
1410 LET B$=A$(4)
1420 FOR I=4 TO 2 STEP -1
1430 LET A$(I)=A$(I-1)
1440 NEXT I
1450 LET A$(1)=B$
1460 RETURN
```

This is the subroutine for the move T which rotates all the squares in a clockwise direction.

```
1500 REM %%%%%%%%%%%%%%%%%%%% EXTRA MOVE FOR MIXING %%%%%%%%%%%%%%%%%%%%
1510 LET B$=A$(3)
1520 FOR I=3 TO 2 STEP -1
1530 LET A$(I)=A$(I-1)
1540 NEXT I
1550 LET A$(1)=B$
1560 RETURN
```

An extra move for mixing the squares. In fact it is the move TTXTTT which moves three of the squares around in a clockwise direction. (Can you work out which three?)

```
1600 REM %%%%%%%%%%%%%%%%%%%% ENDING NOISE EFFECTS %%%%%%%%%%%%%%%%%%%%
1610 POKE 36878,15
1620 FOR L=200 TO 250
1630 POKE 36876,L
1640 FOR I=1 TO 30:NEXT I
1650 NEXT L
1660 POKE 36876,0
1670 POKE 36878,0
1680 RETURN
```

Place your own favourite sound effects here, if available.

See the Appendix for further notes.

```
        FOUR SQUARES
   FOR EXPERIMENT PRESS E
      FOR PUZZLE PRESS P
```

```
         FOUR SQUARES
          CCC   AAA
          CCC   AAA
          CCC   AAA

          DDD   BBB
          DDD   BBB
          DDD   BBB

      X EXCHANGES TOP TWO
      T ROTATES CLOCKWISE
        PRESS * TO END
```

Transpositions. A permutation that interchanges exactly two squares is called a **transposition.** For example, the permutation X, which exchanges the top two squares, is a transposition. The permutation T is not a transposition because it involves moving all four squares. However T is a combination of transpositions. Consider the following sequence of operations:

> exchange the two squares on the top,
> then, exchange the two squares on the left side,
> then, exchange the two squares on the bottom.

This sequence has the same effect as the permutation T. Thus T is indeed the combination of transpositions. In fact every permutation in any group is a combination of transpositions, but we will not go into details.

The program SIXTEEN SQUARES PUZZLE uses the idea of a transposition to produce an interesting computer game. The game is based on the 14-15 puzzle invented by Sam Loyd in the last century. On RUNning the program you will see sixteen squares. Fifteen of these squares have the letters A to O while the sixteenth has some distinguishing symbol such as # or ▓. The object of the game is to place the squares into their correct positions as shown below.

```
A B C D
E F G H
I J K L
M N O #
```

By pressing U, D, R or L you can move the position of the distinguished square. Pressing U exchanges the position of this square with the one immediately above it.

Similarly pressing D, R and L exchanges the distinguished square with the one immediately beneath it, to its right and to its left respectively.

In other words, pressing U, D, R or L performs a transposition.

```
10 REM                   ****************************
20 REM                   *                          *
30 REM                   *  SIXTEEN SQUARES PUZZLE  *
40 REM                   *                          *
50 REM                   ****************************
60 REM
70 REM
100 REM %%%%%%%%%%%%%%%%%%%%%%% SETTING UP %%%%%%%%%%%%%%%%%%%%%%%%%%%%%%%%%%%%
110 LET CS$=CHR$(147) : REM CODE FOR CLEAR SCREEN
120 LET HM$=CHR$(19) : REM CODE FOR HOME
130 LET S=ASC("A") : REM LET S=CODE("A")
140 LET P=4
150 LET Q=4
160 DIM A$(P,Q)
170 FOR I=1 TO P
180 FOR J=1 TO Q
190 LET T=S+Q*(I-1)+(J-1)
200 LET A$(I,J)=CHR$(T)
210 NEXT J
220 NEXT I
230 LET A$(P,Q)="#" : REM LET A$(P,Q)="▩"
240 LET X=P
250 LET Y=Q
```

You can change the "size" of this puzzle by changing the values of P and Q in lines 140 and 150.

```
260 LET M=P
270 LET N=Q
280 PRINT CS$ : REM CLS
290 PRINT "SIXTEEN SQUARES PUZZLE "
300 PRINT
310 PRINT "          WAIT "
400 REM %%%%%%%%%%%%%%%%%%%% MIXING %%%%%%%%%%%%%%%%%%%%%%%%%%%%%%%%%
410 FOR K=1 TO 100
420 LET U=RND(1)
430 IF U<0.25 AND M<P THEN LET M=M+1
440 IF U>=0.25 AND U<0.5 AND M>1 THEN LET M=M-1
450 IF U>=0.5 AND U<0.75 AND N<Q THEN LET N=N+1
460 IF U>=0.75 AND N>1 THEN LET N=N-1
470 GOSUB 1210
480 NEXT K
490 PRINT CS$ : REM CLS
500 GOSUB 1010
600 REM %%%%%%%%%%%%%%%%%%%% YOUR MOVE %%%%%%%%%%%%%%%%%%%%%%%%%%%%%
610 GET G$ : REM LET G$=INKEY$
620 IF G$="*" THEN GOTO 950
630 IF G$<>"D" AND G$<>"U" AND G$<>"R" AND G$<>"L" THEN GOTO 610
640 IF G$="D" AND M<P THEN LET M=M+1
650 IF G$="U" AND M>1 THEN LET M=M-1
660 IF G$="R" AND N<Q THEN LET N=N+1
670 IF G$="L" AND N>1 THEN LET N=N-1
700 REM %%%%%%%%%%%%%%%%%%%% EXCHANGE AND CHECK FOR END %%%%%%%%%%%%%%%%%%
710 REM
720 GOSUB 1210
730 GOSUB 1010
740 LET I=1
750 LET J=P
760 IF I=P AND J=Q THEN GOTO 910
770 LET T=S+Q*(I-1)+(J-1)
780 IF A$(I,J)<>CHR$(T) THEN GOTO 610
790 LET J=J+1
800 IF J>Q THEN LET I=I+1
810 IF J>Q THEN LET J=1
820 IF I<P+1 THEN GOTO 760
900 REM %%%%%%%%%%%%%%%%%%%% ENDING AND ANOTHER GO %%%%%%%%%%%%%%%%%%%%
910 GOSUB 1010
920 PRINT "     WELL DONE"
930 PRINT
940 GOSUB 1310
950 PRINT " ANOTHER GO? Y OR N";
960 GET G$ : REM LET G$=INKEY$
970 IF G$<>"Y" AND G$<>"N" THEN GOTO 960
980 IF G$="Y" THEN GOTO 280
990 END : REM STOP
1000 REM %%%%%%%%%%%%%%%%%%%% PRINT DISPLAY %%%%%%%%%%%%%%%%%%%%%%%%
1010 PRINT HM$ : REM PRINT AT 0,0
1020 PRINT "SIXTEEN SQUARES PUZZLE"
1030 PRINT " U=UP         R=RIGHT"
1040 PRINT
1050 PRINT " D=DOWN       L=LEFT"
1060 PRINT
1070 PRINT
1080 FOR I=1 TO P
```

100 random moves are made. The puzzle is easier if this number is decreased. If you want to see these moves taking place insert an extra line 465 with GOSUB 1010.

A check is made to see if the squares are in their correct positions.

This prints the display.

```
1090 PRINT "        ";
1100 FOR J=1 TO Q
1110 PRINT " ";A$(I,J);
1120 NEXT J
1130 PRINT
1140 PRINT
1150 NEXT I
1160 PRINT
1170 PRINT "   PRESS * TO END"
1180 PRINT
1190 RETURN
1200 REM %%%%%%%%%%%%%%%%%%%%%% EXCHANGE %%%%%%%%%%%%%%%%%%%%%%%%%%%%%%%%
1210 LET B$=A$(M,N)
1220 LET A$(M,N)=A$(X,Y)
1230 LET A$(X,Y)=B$
1240 LET X=M
1250 LET Y=N
1260 RETURN
1300 REM %%%%%%%%%%%%%%%%%%%%%% SOUND EFFECTS %%%%%%%%%%%%%%%%%%%%%%%%%%%
1310 POKE 36878,15
1320 FOR L=200 TO 250
1330 POKE 36876,L
1340 FOR I=1 TO 30:NEXT I
1350 NEXT L
1360 POKE 36876,0:POKE 36878,0
1370 RETURN
```

This subroutine performs the transposition.

Insert your own favourite sound effects here.

See the Appendix for further notes.

```
        SIXTEEN SQUARES PUZZLE

                 WAIT
```

```
           SIXTEEN SQUARES PUZZLE

         U=UP              R=RIGHT

         D=DOWN            L=LEFT


                  F  A  D  G

                  C  B  K  #

                  I  N  O  H

                  M  E  L  J

                PRESS * TO END
```

Cycles. The permutation T "cycles" the four squares in a clockwise direction. We say that T is a **cycle** or a 4-cycle since it cycles four squares around. A transposition is a special kind of cycle; it cycles two squares and so is a 2-cycle. Not every permutation is a cycle. For example, the permutation XTTX exchanges the top two squares with the bottom two - see the diagram.

```
AAA   BBB            CCC   DDD
AAA   BBB            CCC   DDD
AAA   BBB   XTTX     CCC   DDD
                 ⟶
CCC   DDD            AAA   BBB
CCC   DDD            AAA   BBB
CCC   DDD            AAA   BBB
```

This permutation consists of two (disjoint) 2-cycles and hence is not a cycle.

Another example of a cycle is XT which is a 3-cycle because it cycles three of the squares around.

```
AAA  BBB         CCC  BBB
AAA  BBB         CCC  BBB
AAA  BBB   xT    CCC  BBB
              ────▶
CCC  DDD         DDD  AAA
CCC  DDD         DDD  AAA
CCC  DDD         DDD  AAA
```

The concept of a cycle is both important and useful in group theory, although no further details will be given here. The next program TWENTY-FIVE SQUARES PUZZLE uses the idea of cycles to produce an interesting and quite difficult puzzle. It involves permutations of twenty-five squares. The squares are arranged as in the diagram below and are labelled by the twenty-five letters of the alphabet A to Y.

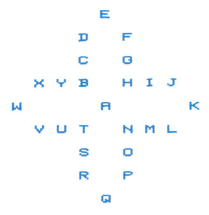

The computer permutes the squares around and you have to rearrange them back into the correct order as shown in the diagram above. Only certain permutations and combinations of them are permitted. These move eight of the squares in either a clockwise or anticlockwise direction. Each permissible move is an 8-cycle. These cycles are effected by pressing the keys 1 to 8. For example, on pressing 3 the eight upper squares are cycled in a clockwise direction. See the diagrams on the next page.

The other moves can be found on RUNning the program.

REARRANGING THINGS

```
            E                           D
        D   F                       C   E
        C   G                       B   F
    X Y B   H I J              X Y A   G I J
W           A       K      W           H       K
    V U T   N M L              V U T   N M L
        S   O                       S   O
        R   P         ──→           R   P
                       3
            Q                           Q


            E                           F
        D   F                       E   G
        C   G                       D   H
    X Y B   H I J              X Y C   A I J
W           A       K      W           B       K
    V U T   N M L              V U T   N M L
        S   O                       S   O
        R   P         ──→           R   P
                       4
            Q                           Q


            E                           E
        D   F                       D   F
        C   G                       C   G
    X Y B   H I J              X Y B   H I J
W           A       K      W           T       K
    V U T   N M L              V U S   A M L
        S   O                       R   N
        R   P         ──→           Q   O
                       7
            Q                           P
```

REARRANGING THINGS

```
10 REM
20 REM             ********************************
30 REM             *                                *
40 REM             *  TWENTY-FIVE SQUARES PUZZLE   *
50 REM             *                                *
60 REM             ********************************
70 REM
100 REM %%%%%%%%%%%%%%%%%%%%% SETTING UP %%%%%%%%%%%%%%%%%%%%%%%%%%%%%%
110 LET CS$=CHR$(147) : REM CODE FOR CLEAR SCREEN
120 LET HM$=CHR$(19) : REM CODE FOR HOME
130 LET I$=CHR$(18)
140 LET O$=CHR$(146)
150 DIM A$(25)
160 LET S=ASC("A")-1 : REM LET S=CODE("A")-1
170 FOR I=1 TO 25
180 LET A$(I)=I$+CHR$(S+I)+O$
190 REM FOR ZX81 USE   LET A$(I)=CHR$(128+S+I)
200 NEXT I
```

I$ stands for "reverse video on" (or "inverse video on") while O$ stands for "reverse video off". See the Appendix.

A$(I) stores the 25 letters of the alphabet A-Y.

```
300 REM %%%%%%%%%%%%%%%%%%%%% INITIAL DISPLAY %%%%%%%%%%%%%%%%%%%%%%%%
310 PRINT CS$; : REM CLS
320 PRINT "     25 SQUARES"
330 GOSUB 810
340 PRINT
350 PRINT " C=CLOCKWISE   A=ANTI"
360 PRINT "    PRESS * TO END"
400 REM %%%%%%%%%%%%%%%%%%%%% MIXING %%%%%%%%%%%%%%%%%%%%%%%%%%%%%%%%%
410 FOR J=1 TO 25
420 ON INT(8*RND(1)+1)GOSUB 1110,1210,1310,1410,1510,1610,1710,1810
430 REM GOSUB 1110+INT(RND*8)*100
440 NEXT J
450 GOSUB 810
```

To see the random moves taking place, interchange lines 440 and 450.

```
500 REM %%%%%%%%%%%%%%%%%%%%% YOUR MOVE %%%%%%%%%%%%%%%%%%%%%%%%%%%%%%
510 GET G$ : REM LET G$=INKEY$
520 IF G$="*" THEN GOTO 670
530 IF G$<"1" OR G$>"8" THEN GOTO 510
540 ON VAL(G$) GOSUB 1110,1210,1310,1410,1510,1610,1710,1810
550 REM GOSUB 1010+100*VAL(G$)
560 GOSUB 810
600 REM %%%%%%%%%%%%%%%%%%%%% CHECKING FOR END AND ANOTHER GO %%%%%%%%%%%%
610 LET J=1
620 IF A$(J)<>I$+CHR$(S+J)+O$ THEN GOTO 510
630 REM IF A$(J)<>CHR$(128+S+J) THEN GOTO 510
640 LET J=J+1
650 IF J<26 THEN GOTO 620
660 GOSUB 1910
670 PRINT
680 PRINT "  ANOTHER GO? Y OR N"
690 GET G$ : REM LET G$=INKEY$
700 IF G$<>"Y" AND G$<>"N" THEN GOTO 690
710 IF G$="Y" THEN GOTO 310
720 END : REM STOP
```

```
800 REM %%%%%%%%%%%%%%%%%%%%%% DISPLAY %%%%%%%%%%%%%%%%%%%%%%%%%%%%%%%
810 PRINT HM$ : REM PRINT AT 0,0
820 PRINT
830 PRINT TAB(10);A$(5)
840 PRINT
850 PRINT TAB(8);A$(4);" 3 ";A$(6)
860 PRINT TAB(10);"C"
870 PRINT TAB(8);A$(3);"   ";A$(7)
880 PRINT TAB(10);"4"
890 PRINT TAB(4);A$(24);" ";A$(25);" ";A$(2);" A ";A$(8);" ";
900 PRINT A$(9);" ";A$(10)
910 PRINT
920 PRINT TAB(2);A$(23);" 1C 2A ";A$(1);" 5C 6A ";A$(11)
930 PRINT
940 PRINT TAB(4);A$(22);" ";A$(21);" ";A$(20);" 7 ";A$(14);
950 PRINT " ";A$(13);" ";A$(12)
960 PRINT TAB(10);"C"
970 PRINT TAB(8);A$(19);"   ";A$(15)
980 PRINT TAB(10);"8"
990 PRINT TAB(8);A$(18);" A ";A$(16)
1000 PRINT
1010 PRINT TAB(10);A$(17)
1020 RETURN
1100 REM %%%%%%%%%%%%%%%%%%%%%% MOVE 1 - LEFT CLOCKWISE %%%%%%%%%%%%%%%%%%%
1110 LET B$=A$(25)
1120 FOR I=25 TO 21 STEP -1
1130 LET A$(I)=A$(I-1)
1140 NEXT I
1150 LET A$(20)=A$(1)
1160 LET A$(1)=A$(2)
1170 LET A$(2)=B$
1180 RETURN
1200 REM %%%%%%%%%%%%%%%%%%%%%% MOVE 2 - LEFT ANTICLOCKWISE %%%%%%%%%%%%%%%
1210 LET B$=A$(20)
1220 FOR I=20 TO 24
1230 LET A$(I)=A$(I+1)
1240 NEXT I
1250 LET A$(25)=A$(2)
1260 LET A$(2)=A$(1)
1270 LET A$(1)=B$
1280 RETURN
1300 REM %%%%%%%%%%%%%%%%%%%%%% MOVE 3 - UP CLOCKWISE %%%%%%%%%%%%%%%%%%%%%
1310 LET B$=A$(8)
1320 FOR I=8 TO 2 STEP -1
1330 LET A$(I)=A$(I-1)
1340 NEXT I
1350 LET A$(1)=B$
1360 RETURN
1400 REM %%%%%%%%%%%%%%%%%%%%%% MOVE 4 - UP ANTICLOCKWISE %%%%%%%%%%%%%%%%%
1410 LET B$=A$(1)
1420 FOR I=1 TO 7
1430 LET A$(I)=A$(I+1)
1440 NEXT I
1450 LET A$(8)=B$
1460 RETURN
```

```
1500 REM %%%%%%%%%%%%%%%%%%%% MOVE 5 - RIGHT CLOCKWISE %%%%%%%%%%%%%%%%%%%%
1510 LET B$=A$(14)
1520 FOR I=14 TO 9 STEP -1
1530 LET A$(I)=A$(I-1)
1540 NEXT I
1550 LET A$(8)=A$(1)
1560 LET A$(1)=B$
1570 RETURN
1600 REM %%%%%%%%%%%%%%%%%%%% MOVE 6 - RIGHT ANTICLOCKWISE %%%%%%%%%%%%%%%%
1610 LET B$=A$(8)
1620 FOR I=8 TO 13
1630 LET A$(I)=A$(I+1)
1640 NEXT I
1650 LET A$(14)=A$(1)
1660 LET A$(1)=B$
1670 RETURN
1700 REM %%%%%%%%%%%%%%%%%%%% MOVE 7 - DOWN CLOCKWISE %%%%%%%%%%%%%%%%%%%%%
1710 LET B$=A$(20)
1720 FOR I=20 TO 15 STEP -1
1730 LET A$(I)=A$(I-1)
1740 NEXT I
1750 LET A$(14)=A$(1)
1760 LET A$(1)=B$
1770 RETURN
1800 REM %%%%%%%%%%%%%%%%%%%% MOVE 8 - DOWN ANTICLOCKWISE %%%%%%%%%%%%%%%%%
1810 LET B$=A$(14)
1820 FOR I=14 TO 19
1830 LET A$(I)=A$(I+1)
1840 NEXT I
1850 LET A$(20)=A$(1)
1860 LET A$(1)=B$
1870 RETURN
1900 REM %%%%%%%%%%%%%%%%%%%% ENDING NOISE EFFECTS %%%%%%%%%%%%%%%%%%%%%%%%
1910 POKE 36878,15
1920 FOR L=200 TO 250
1930 POKE 36876,L
1940 FOR I=1 TO 30
1950 NEXT I
1960 NEXT L
1970 POKE 36876,0
1980 POKE 36878,0
1990 RETURN
```

Place your own sound effects here, if available.

See the Appendix for further notes.

```
               25 SQUARES
                   A
             L  `3  E
                 C
             I      J
                 4
          W  X  N  A  K  V  M

       C  1C  2A  T  5C  6A  P

          F  Y  Q  7  U  G  S
                 C
                O     B
                 8
                H A  D

                   R
         C=CLOCKWISE   A=ANTI
            PRESS * TO END
```

For more details about the various concepts associated with groups you may like to consult Puzzle it Out: Cubes, Groups and Puzzles by John Ewing and Czes Kosniowski.

WAIT

about the theory of queues or lines

How many times have you been in a supermarket or post office, seen a number of lines or **queues**, stood in one and discovered that it is the one queue that is not moving because of some difficult customer in front. Queues infuriate us, and no doubt we spend a good deal of our time waiting in queues.

One way to avoid the problem of several queues is to have just one queue which feeds the assistants on a first come first served basis. Many banks and post offices now adopt this system.

Suppose we have such a situation, say in a bank, with one or more assistants serving. The customers form a single queue and are served on a first come first served basis by the assistants. Customers do not usually come at regular intervals. If on average there are 10 customers per hour, which is 1 customer per six minutes, then we certainly would not expect exactly one customer every six minutes. The difference between the time of arrival of one customer and another is called the **inter-arrival time**. Regardless of the number of people in a queue the inter-arrival times between incoming customers are random events.

We can use our microcomputer to "simulate" the arrival times of customers. Such a simulation process is often referred to as a **Monte-Carlo** process. This is illustrated by a simple example. If the average number of customers arriving is one every six minutes then there is, approximately, a one-in-six chance that a customer arrives during any given one minute interval. Thus each minute our microcomputer could choose a random number (between 0 and 1) and check to see if it is less than 1/6. If it is then we say that a customer has arrived and otherwise not. Of course we speed things up and do not literally let the computer make a choice every minute.

The first few minutes of such a process are illustrated in the table below.

Time (minutes)	Random number, RND	Less than 1/6?	Customer arrival time
1	0.21273	No	-
2	0.10601	Yes	2
3	0.31993	No	-
4	0.65851	No	-
5	0.66965	No	-
6	0.97381	No	-
7	0.59476	No	-
8	0.50985	No	-
9	0.42101	No	-
10	0.52048	No	-
11	0.09276	Yes	11
.	.	.	.
.	.	.	.
.	.	.	.

The program CUSTOMER ARRIVALS I runs through a sixty minute time span and prints out the arrival time of each new customer. The assumption is that on average there is a new customer every six minutes; in other words the customer arrival rate (CAR) is 1/6 per minute.

```
10 REM                  **********************
20 REM                  *                    *
30 REM                  * CUSTOMER ARRIVALS I *
40 REM                  *                    *
50 REM                  **********************
60 REM
70 REM
100 REM %%%%%%%%%%%%%%%%%%%%% SETTING UP %%%%%%%%%%%%%%%%%%%%%%%%%%%%
110 LET CAR=1/6 : REM CUSTOMER ARRIVAL RATE
120 REM SEE WARNING IN TEXT
130 LET T=60 : REM TOTAL TIME INTERVAL
140 PRINT CHR$(147) : REM CLEAR SCREEN
150 PRINT " CUSTOMER ARRIVALS I"
200 REM %%%%%%%%%%%%%%%%%%%%% CALCULATE AND PRINT %%%%%%%%%%%%%%%%%%%%%%%
210 PRINT
220 PRINT "    ARRIVAL RATE"
230 PRINT CAR;"PER MINUTE"
240 PRINT
250 PRINT "    TIME OF ARRIVAL "
260 PRINT " MINUTES AFTER START"
```

```
270 PRINT
280 LET K=0
290 FOR I=1 TO T
300 LET X=RND(1)
310 IF X<CAR THEN PRINT "        ";I
320 IF X<CAR THEN LET K=K+1
330 NEXT I
340 PRINT
350 PRINT "TOTAL CUSTOMERS ";K
360 PRINT
370 PRINT " ANOTHER GO? Y OR N"
380 GET G$ : REM LET G$=INKEY$
390 IF G$<>"Y" ANDG$<>"N" THEN GOTO 380
400 IF G$="Y" THEN GOTO 210
```

See the Appendix for some general notes.

```
          CUSTOMER ARRIVALS  I

              ARRIVAL RATE
           .166666667 PER MINUTE

              TIME OF ARRIVAL
           MINUTES AFTER START

                    7
                   12
                   14
                   18
                   25
                   30
                   33
                   35
                   36
                   37

         TOTAL CUSTOMERS    10

         ANOTHER GO?   Y OR N
```

You have to be careful when writing a program such as CUSTOMER ARRIVALS I. What if the average number of customers arriving is one per minute? You cannot just change the value of CAR in line 110 to the number 1. If you did you would get exactly one customer every minute, which is not very likely in real life. (This partly explains why the word approximately was used earlier on.) To get around this problem we choose a smaller time interval, for example one-tenth of a minute. Now the likelihood of a customer arriving in a given one-tenth of a minute is approximately 1/10.

In general you should choose your time interval to be as small as possible. Decreasing the time interval increases the number of calculations that need to be performed. The program CUSTOMER ARRIVALS II incorporates these suggestions.

```
10 REM                  **************************
20 REM                  *                        *
30 REM                  * CUSTOMER ARRIVALS II  *
40 REM                  *                        *
50 REM                  **************************
60 REM
70 REM
100 REM %%%%%%%%%%%%%%%%%%%%%% SETTING UP %%%%%%%%%%%%%%%%%%%%%%%%%%%%%%
110 LET CAR=1/6 : REM CUSTOMER ARRIVAL RATE
120 LET R=1
130 LET R=R/10
140 LET S=CAR*R
150 IF S>0.1 THEN GOTO 130
160 LET T=60 : REM TOTAL TIME INTERVAL
170 PRINT CHR$(147) : REM CLEAR SCREEN
180 PRINT " CUSTOMER ARRIVALS II"
```

The time interval is continually divided by 10 until the likelihood of a customer arriving during this time interval is at most 1/10.

```
200 REM %%%%%%%%%%%%%%%%%%%%%% CALCULATE AND PRINT %%%%%%%%%%%%%%%%%%%%
210 PRINT
220 PRINT "     ARRIVAL RATE"
230 PRINT CAR;"PER MINUTE"
240 PRINT
250 PRINT "    TIME OF ARRIVAL"
260 PRINT " MINUTES AFTER START"
270 PRINT
280 LET K=0
290 FOR I=1 TO T STEP R
300 LET X=RND(1)
310 IF X<S THEN PRINT "          ";INT(I*10)/10
320 IF X<S THEN LET K=K+1
330 NEXT I
340 PRINT
350 PRINT "TOTAL CUSTOMERS ";K
360 PRINT
370 PRINT " ANOTHER GO?  Y OR N"
380 GET G$ : REM LET G$=INKEY$
390 IF G$<>"Y" AND G$<>"N" THEN GOTO 380
400 IF G$="Y" THEN GOTO 210
```

See the Appendix for further notes.

```
          CUSTOMER ARRIVALS II

               ARRIVAL RATE
           .16666667 PER MINUTE

              TIME OF ARRIVAL
           MINUTES AFTER START

                   2.8
                  15.5
                  20.6
                  26.3
                  27.7
                  34.5
                  36.1
                  45.9
                  55.7

           TOTAL CUSTOMERS   9

           ANOTHER GO?  Y OR N
```

There is an alternative to this approach which tends to speed up the calculations. We use the random numbers to determine the inter-arrival times between customers. Suppose that CAR is the customer arrival rate. The number CAR does not have to be a whole number! It turns out that the likelihood or probability that the inter-arrival time is less than or equal to Y is given by the formula 1 - EXP(-CAR*Y).

For example, there is a 0.632 (i.e. 63.2%) chance of a customer arriving within the time 1/CAR after another customer. (On average there is one customer in the time 1/CAR, but customers do not arrive regularly.)

The graph of 1 - EXP(-CAR*Y) with varying Y is given on the next page.

Observe that, as expected, the probability of the inter-arrival time being 0 is 0. Also, the probability of the inter-arrival time being less than some very large number is about 1.

The formula given above is called the **probability distribution function** or the **cumulative distribution function.** The justification for the formula will not be given but experience has shown that it fits observations very

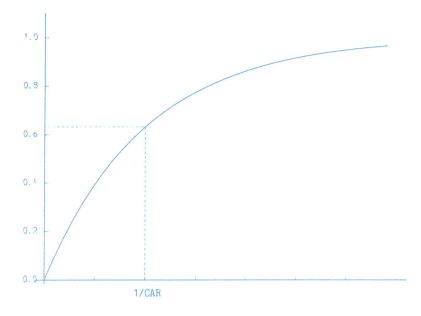

Graph of 1 - EXP(CAR*Y)

well. It is based on the so-called **Poisson** arrival of customers. This briefly means that the customers arrive randomly but with a fixed probability of arriving during any small time interval. You may have heard of the name Poisson before; S. D. Poisson (1781-1840) was a French mathematician and physicist who is noted for several contributions to mechanics and electrostatics.

Using the above formula your microcomputer can simulate the arrival times of customers. First note that 1 - EXP(-CAR*Y) is a number between 0 and 1. The inter-arrival time of a random customer can be found by choosing a random number RND (between 0 and 1), calculating 1 - RND, and then comparing the result with 1 - EXP(-CAR*Y). Using some easy algebra we have the following equations.

$$1 - EXP(-CAR*Y) = 1 - RND$$
$$EXP(-CAR*Y) = RND$$
$$-CAR*Y = LN(RND)$$
$$Y = -LN(RND)/CAR$$

Thus the random number RND determines the inter-arrival time Y by the formula Y = -LN(RND)/CAR.

For example, suppose that CAR is 1/6. The first few arrivals are calculated as in the table below.

Random number, RND	Inter-arrival time, -LN(RND)/CAR	Customer arrival time
0.81785	1.21	1.21
0.18753	10.04	11.25
0.54975	3.59	14.84
0.38481	5.73	20.57
0.05226	17.71	38.28
0.23964	8.57	46.85
0.69152	2.21	49.06
0.56127	3.47	52.53
0.79813	1.35	53.88
0.81238	1.25	55.13
.	.	.
.	.	.
.	.	.

The program CUSTOMER ARRIVALS III uses the formula just mentioned to simulate customers arriving during a sixty minute period. The customer arrival rate is 1/6. You can change the period and the average arrival rate if you want to.

```
10 REM                    ***************************
20 REM                    *                         *
30 REM                    * CUSTOMER ARRIVALS III *
40 REM                    *                         *
50 REM                    ***************************
60 REM
70 REM
100 REM %%%%%%%%%%%%%%%%%%%% SETTING UP %%%%%%%%%%%%%%%%%%%%%%%%%%%%
110 LET CAR=1/6 : REM CUSTOMER ARRIVAL RATE
130 LET T=60 : REM TOTAL TIME INTERVAL
140 PRINT CHR$(147) : REM CLEAR SCREEN
150 PRINT "CUSTOMER ARRIVALS III"
200 REM %%%%%%%%%%%%%%%%%%% CALCULATE AND PRINT %%%%%%%%%%%%%%%%%%%
210 PRINT
220 PRINT "    ARRIVAL RATE"
230 PRINT CAR;"PER MINUTE"
240 PRINT
250 PRINT "   TIME OF ARRIVAL"
```

```
260 PRINT " MINUTES AFTER START"
270 PRINT
280 LET K=0
290 LET Z=0
300 LET X=RND(1)
310 LET Y=-LOG(X)/CAR : REM INTER-ARRIVAL TIME
320 LET Y=INT(100*Y+0.5)/100
330 LET Z=Z+Y
340 IF Z>T THEN GOTO 380
350 PRINT "          ";Z
360 LET K=K+1
370 GOTO 300
380 PRINT
390 PRINT "TOTAL CUSTOMERS ";K
400 PRINT
410 PRINT " ANOTHER GO?  Y OR N"
420 GET G$ : REM LET G$=INKEY$
430 IF G$<>"Y" AND G$<>"N" THEN GOTO 420
440 IF G$="Y" THEN GOTO 210
```

See the Appendix for general notes.

```
        CUSTOMER ARRIVALS III

             ARRIVAL RATE
         .166666667 PER MINUTE

            TIME OF ARRIVAL
         MINUTES AFTER START

                  18.95
                  19.63
                  29.43
                  33.78
                  34.42
                  40.3
                  57
                  57.94
                  58.52
                  58.72

         TOTAL CUSTOMERS   10

            ANOTHER GO?  Y OR N
```

Notice that CUSTOMER ARRIVALS I requires 60 random numbers, while CUSTOMER ARRIVALS II requires about 600. On the other hand, CUSTOMER ARRIVALS III requires only about 10.

Customers do not arrive at regular intervals. Equally, assistants do not serve each customer in the same amount of time. The time taken usually varies from customer to customer. This time is given by a formula similar to the one for the inter-arrival time of customers. Indeed, if CSR is the customer service rate (the average number of customers that an assistant can deal with) then the probability that a customer is served within time Y is 1 - EXP(-CSR*Y). Using technical words we say that the time it takes to serve customers has an **exponential distribution.** We can simulate the time taken to serve customers in a manner similar to the inter-arrival rate of customers, simply by replacing CAR with CSR.

Both processes can be combined. We can then simulate what happens in the situation of a single queue being served by one or more assistants. This gives a good insight into any potential problems that may arise without the expense or danger of working with real customers and assistants.

The program BANK QUEUES simulates one week at a bank operating with one or more assistants. The week is broken up into 6 days of 360 minutes (6 hours). Each day the bank is open from 10.00 a.m. to 4.00 p.m. (or using the 24 hour clock, from 1000 to 1600). There is only one queue for the customers who are served on a first come first served basis. The customer arrival rate is 24 per hour, while the assistants can deal with a customer, on average, in 10 minutes. These rates may be changed if you want a busier bank.

On RUNning the program you will be asked for the number of assistants you want each day. The bank is quite small and any queue formed must not become too long. You will be asked for the maximum number of customers that can queue in the bank, this number does not include the customers being served. After this you will be given a minute by minute account (speeded up) of how the bank is managing. At the end of each day a summary is given for that day and any preceeding days. This summary gives the number of assistants, the maximum number of customers allowed in a queue, the number of customers lost because the queue was full up and the average time during the 360 minutes that an assistant was serving customers. This last figure gives you information on how busy each assistant was.

For convenience it is assumed that the assistants have no lunch breaks etc. Also, once the 360 minutes are up then all customers, except those being served, are thrown out. The number thrown out is included in the number of lost customers. Note that it is possible for the assistants to serve for more than 360 minutes. This happens if the assistants are busy all the time and continue serving a customer once the bank is closed.

Experiment to see how small your bank can be and how mean you can be on the number of assistants.

```
10 REM                        **************
20 REM                        *            *
30 REM                        * BANK QUEUES *
40 REM                        *            *
50 REM                        **************
60 REM
70 REM
100 REM %%%%%%%%%%%%%%%%%%%%%% SETTING UP %%%%%%%%%%%%%%%%%%%%%%%%%%%%%%
110 LET C$=CHR$(147) : REM CODE FOR CLEAR SCREEN
120 LET HM$=CHR$(19) : REM CODE FOR HOME
130 LET CAR=0.4 : REM CUSTOMER ARRIVAL RATE
140 LET CSR=0.1 : REM CUSTOMER SERVICE RATE
150 DIM A(10)
160 DIM S(6)
170 DIM T(6)          You can change the values of CAR and CSR if you wish.
180 DIM L(6)
190 DIM M(6)
```

The array A(I) stores the time that an assistant will finish with a customer. The number of assistants on each of the six days is stored in S(I). The array T(I) stores the total time that the assistants serve on each of the six days. L(I) keeps track of the number of lost customers each day and finally M(I) stores the maximum number of customers allowed in a queue.

```
200 LET DAY=1
210 LET B$=CHR$(31) : REM BLUE
220 LET R$=CHR$(28) : REM RED
230 LET M$=CHR$(156) : REM MAGENTA OR PURPLE
240 LET G$=CHR$(30) : REM GREEN
250 LET C$=CHR$(159) : REM CYAN
260 LET Y$=CHR$(158) : REM YELLOW
```

If colours are available on your computer then put in the appropriate code numbers; otherwise delete B$, R$, etc.

```
300 REM %%%%%%%%%%%%%%%%%%%%%% START OF DAY %%%%%%%%%%%%%%%%%%%%%%%%%%%
310 PRINT CS$ : REM CLS
320 PRINT R$+"        BANK QUEUES"
330 PRINT
340 PRINT B$+"         DAY ";DAY
```

WAIT

```
350 PRINT
360 PRINT "ARRIVAL RATE = 24/HOUR"
370 PRINT "SERVICE RATE =  6/HOUR"
380 PRINT M$+" NUMBER OF ASSISTANTS"
390 PRINT M$+" REQUIRED TODAY? 1-10"
400 PRINT B$
410 INPUT AS
420 LET AS=INT(AS+0.5)
430 IF AS<1 OR AS>10 THEN GOTO 410
440 LET S(DAY)=AS
450 PRINT
460 PRINT M$+" MAXIMUM QUEUE LENGTH"
470 PRINT " ALLOWED?"
480 PRINT B$
490 INPUT MAX
500 LET MAX=INT(MAX+0.5)
510 LET M(DAY)=MAX
520 FOR I=1 TO AS
530 LET A(I)=0
540 NEXT I
600 REM %%%%%%%%%%%%%%%%%%%%% DAYS EVENTS %%%%%%%%%%%%%%%%%%%%%%%%%%
610 PRINT CS$ : REM CLS
620 PRINT R$+"      BANK QUEUES"
630 PRINT
640 PRINT "DAY";DAY;" OPEN 1000-1600"
650 PRINT
660 PRINT "ASSISTANTS: ";AS
670 PRINT
680 LET LC=0 : REM LOST CUSTOMERS
690 LET TT=0 : REM TOTAL TIME ASSISTANTS SERVE
700 LET Q=0  : REM LENGTH OF QUEUE
710 LET T=0  : REM TIME IN MINUTES
720 GOSUB 1510
800 REM %%%%%%%%%%%%%%%%%%%%% MINUTE BY MINUTE %%%%%%%%%%%%%%%%%%%%%
810 FOR T=1 TO 360
820 IF T>TA THEN GOSUB 1510
830 LET TS=0 : REM NUMBER OF ASSISTANTS SERVING
840 FOR J=1 TO AS
850 IF Q>0 AND A(J)<=T THEN GOSUB 1710
860 IF A(J)>T THEN LET TS=TS+1
870 NEXT J
880 LET P=7
890 GOSUB 1810
900 PRINT G$+"TIME: ";1000+T+40*INT(T/60)
910 PRINT
920 PRINT B$+"CUSTOMERS WAITING";STR$(Q);" "
930 PRINT
940 PRINT M$+"ASSISTANTS SERVING";STR$(TS);" "
950 PRINT
960 PRINT Y$+"CUSTOMERS LOST";LC
970 PRINT
980 PRINT C$+"TOTAL TIME"
990 PRINT C$+"SPENT SERVING ";TT
1000 NEXT T
1100 REM %%%%%%%%%%%%%%%%%%%%% END OF DAY SUMMARY %%%%%%%%%%%%%%%%%%
1110 LET T(DAY)=INT(TT/AS+.5)
1120 LET L(DAY)=LC+Q
1130 PRINT CS$ : REM CLS
```

This INPUTs the number of assistants required and the maximum number of queueing customers.

This calculates the minute by minute state of customers arriving and assistants serving.

```
1140 PRINT R$+"  QUEUES - SUMMARY"
1150 PRINT
1160 PRINT B$+"ARRIVAL RATE = 24/HOUR"
1170 PRINT B$+"SERVICE RATE =  6/HOUR"
1180 PRINT R$+"ASSTS MAX  LOST  AV "
1190 PRINT R$+"          Q   CUST TIME"
1200 PRINT
1210 FOR I=1 TO DAY
1220 PRINT TAB(3-LEN(STR$(S(I))));S(I);
1230 PRINT TAB(9-LEN(STR$(M(I))));M(I);
1240 PRINT TAB(13-LEN(STR$(L(I))));L(I);
1250 PRINT TAB(20-LEN(STR$(T(I))));T(I)
1260 NEXT I
1270 PRINT
1280 PRINT G$+"  PRESS Y TO GO ON"
1290 GET H$ : REM LET H$=INKEY$
1300 IF H$<>"Y" THEN GOTO 1290
1310 LET DAY=DAY+1
1320 IF DAY<7 THEN GOTO 310
1400 REM %%%%%%%%%%%%%%%%%% ANOTHER WEEK? %%%%%%%%%%%%%%%%%%
1410 PRINT
1420 PRINT G$+" ANOTHER WEEK? Y OR N"
1430 GET H$ : REM LET H$=INKEY$
1440 IF H$<>"Y" AND H$<>"N" THEN GOTO 1430
1450 IF H$="Y" THEN GOTO 200
1460 END : REM STOP
1500 REM %%%%%%%%%%%%%%%%%% TIME OF NEXT CUSTOMER %%%%%%%%%%%%%%%%%%
1510 LET Q=Q+1
1520 LET TA=T-LOG(RND(1))/CAR
1530 IF Q<=MAX THEN RETURN
1540 REM %%%%%%%%%% LOST CUSTOMERS %%%%%%%%%%
1550 LET Q=MAX
1560 LET P=18
1570 GOSUB 1810
1580 PRINT Y$+"     LONG QUEUE"
1590 PRINT Y$+"   CUSTOMER  LOST"+B$
1600 FOR I=1 TO 200
1610 NEXT I
1620 LET P=18
1630 GOSUB 1810
1640 PRINT "                    "
1650 PRINT "                    "
1660 LET LC=LC+1
1670 RETURN
1700 REM %%%%%%%%%%%%%%%%%% ASSISTANTS SERVING TIME %%%%%%%%%%%%%%%%%%
1710 LET Q=Q-1
1720 LET SA=LOG(RND(1))/CSR
1730 LET A(J)=T-SA
1740 LET TT=TT-INT(SA)
1750 RETURN
1800 REM %%%%%%%%%%%%%%%%%% PRINT P LINES %%%%%%%%%%%%%%%%%%
1805 REM PRINT AT P,0
1810 PRINT HM$;
1820 FOR I=1 TO P
1830 PRINT
1840 NEXT I
1850 RETURN
```

A summary of each day is printed.

See the Appendix for further notes.

The time of arrival of the next customer is calculated.

If the queue exceeds the maximum length then a message is flashed.

The service time is calculated.

This is used to determine the line of printing. Use PRINT AT P,0 etc., if available.

```
        BANK QUEUES

          DAY   1

  ARRIVAL RATE = 24/HOUR

  SERVICE RATE =  6/HOUR

   NUMBER OF ASSISTANTS
   REQUIRED TODAY? 1-10

  ? 2

   MAXIMUM QUEUE LENGTH
   ALLOWED?

  ? 3
```

```
         BANK QUEUES

  DAY 1   OPEN 1000-1600

  ASSISTANTS:   2

  TIME:   1220

  CUSTOMERS WAITING 3

  ASSISTANTS SERVING 2

  CUSTOMERS LOST 14

  TOTAL TIME
  SPENT SERVING   252

        LONG QUEUE
      CUSTOMER  LOST
```

```
        QUEUES - SUMMARY
      ARRIVAL RATE = 24/HOUR
      SERVICE RATE =  6/HOUR
      ASSTS  MAX   LOST    AV
               Q   CUST   TIME
         2     3    38    365
         3     5    25    340
         4     6     6    309
         2     2    47    342
         1     5    81    364
         6     3     0    214
         PRESS Y TO GO ON
```

There are formulae which will tell you what will happen to a queue, but they tend to take some of the fun out of looking at queues. The program QUEUE ANALYSIS performs the necessary calculations and tells you the average length of the queue.

When you RUN the program you will be asked to INPUT the customer arrival rate (CAR), the customer service rate (CSR) and the number of assistants (AS). If the number of assistants is less than CAR/CSR then the queue quickly becomes very long and unmanagable. The expected average length of the queue EQ is printed out.

You could incorporate some other calculations in this program. For example, the expected average time that a customer spends waiting in the queue is EQ/CAR. The average time that a customer spends in the queue and in being served is EQ/CAR + 1/CSR. Finally, the average number of customers is EQ + CAR/CSR.

```
10 REM                  *******************
20 REM                  *                 *
30 REM                  * QUEUE ANALYSIS  *
40 REM                  *                 *
50 REM                  *******************
60 REM
70 REM
100 REM %%%%%%%%%%%%%%%%%%%%%% SETTING UP %%%%%%%%%%%%%%%%%%%%%%%%%%%
110 DIM F(10) : REM FACTORIALS
120 LET F(0)=1                          The factorials required are cal-
130 FOR I=1 TO 10                       culated here.
140 LET F(I)=I*F(I-1)
150 NEXT I
200 REM %%%%%%%%%%%%%%%%%%%%%% INPUT DATA %%%%%%%%%%%%%%%%%%%%%%%%%%
210 PRINT CHR$(147) : REM CLEAR SCREEN
220 PRINT "   QUEUE ANALYSIS"
230 PRINT
240 PRINT "FOR UPTO 10 ASSISTANTS"
250 PRINT
260 PRINT "CUSTOMER ARRIVAL"
270 PRINT "RATE";
280 INPUT CAR                           This section INPUTs the required
290 PRINT                               data.
300 PRINT "CUSTOMER SERVICE"
310 PRINT "RATE";
320 INPUT CSR
330 PRINT
340 PRINT "NUMBER OF"
350 PRINT "ASSISTANTS";
360 INPUT AS
370 LET AS=INT(AS+0.5)
380 IF AS<1 OR AS>10 THEN GOTO 360
390 PRINT
400 REM %%%%%%%%%%%%%%%%%%%%%% CALCULATING %%%%%%%%%%%%%%%%%%%%%%%%%
410 IF CSR<=0 THEN GOTO 650
420 LET X=CAR/CSR
430 IF AS<=X THEN GOTO 650
440 LET P1=0
450 FOR K=0 TO AS-1                     The expected queue length is
460 LET P1=P1+X↑K/F(K)                  calculated.
470 NEXT K
480 LET P1=P1+X↑AS*AS/(F(AS)*(AS-X))
490 LET E=(AS-X)*(AS-X)*F(AS-1)*P1
500 LET EQ=X↑(AS+1)/E
510 LET EQ=INT(EQ+0.5)
600 REM %%%%%%%%%%%%%%%%%%%%%% DISPLAY %%%%%%%%%%%%%%%%%%%%%%%%%%%%%
610 PRINT "EXPECTED NUMBER OF"
620 PRINT "CUSTOMERS WAITING"
630 PRINT "IN QUEUE: ";EQ
640 GOTO 670
650 PRINT "QUEUE WILL BECOME"            See the Appendix for further notes.
660 PRINT "VERY    L O N G"
670 PRINT
680 PRINT " ANOTHER GO? Y OR N"
690 GET G$ : REM LET G$=INKEY$
700 IF G$<>"Y"AND G$<>"N" THEN GOTO 690
710 IF G$="Y" THEN GOTO 210
```

```
       QUEUE  ANALYSIS

  FOR UPTO 10 ASSISTANTS

  CUSTOMER  ARRIVAL
  RATE? 24

  CUSTOMER  SERVICE
  RATE? 6

  NUMBER OF
  ASSISTANTS? 3

  QUEUE WILL BECOME
  VERY   L O N G

     ANOTHER GO? Y OR N
```

```
       QUEUE  ANALYSIS

  FOR UPTO 10 ASSISTANTS

  CUSTOMER  ARRIVAL
  RATE? 24

  CUSTOMER  SERVICE
  RATE? 6

  NUMBER OF
  ASSISTANTS? 5

  EXPECTED NUMBER OF
  CUSTOMERS WAITING
  IN QUEUE:   2

     ANOTHER GO? Y OR N
```

WAIT

By introducing some extra factors into BANK QUEUES we can produce an interesting computer game called BOUTIQUEUES. This concerns queues at a boutique.

In BOUTIQUEUES you own a boutique which is open for 6 hours a day, 6 days a week. Each day the shop is open from 1000 to 1600, that is from 10.00 a.m. to 4.00 p.m. You hire assistants on a daily basis. Assisitants are very expensive. Each assistant costs $200 a day and can serve customers at an average rate of 9 per hour. When being served by an assistant, each customer spends about $1.50 per minute.

Initially, customers are expected to arrive at the rate of 6 per hour. However, by advertising (at a cost of $100) you can increase the customer arrival rate by 6 per hour. In addition, by offering a 10% discount to all customers you can increase the customer arrival rate by a further 6 per hour. Thus, for example, if on the first day you advertised and offered a 10% discount then the expected rate of arrival of customers will be 18 per hour. (The customer service rate always remains at 9 per hour.)

Customers do not like to be kept waiting. They will join a queue only if it is a short one. If the queue is too long the customer goes away - very disgruntled. In fact so disgruntled that word quickly spreads to other potential customers. The result is that the customer arrival rate is decreased by about 10%.

The object of the game is to make as much profit as you can in a week.

```
10 REM                    ***************
20 REM                    *             *
30 REM                    * BOUTIQUEUES *
40 REM                    *             *
50 REM                    ***************
60 REM
70 REM
100 REM %%%%%%%%%%%%%%%%%%%% SETTING UP %%%%%%%%%%%%%%%%%%%%%%%%%%%%%
110 LET CS$=CHR$(147) : REM CODE FOR CLEAR SCREEN
120 LET HM$=CHR$(19)  : REM CODE FOR HOME
125 LET B$=CHR$(31)   : REM BLUE
127 LET R$=CHR$(28)   : REM RED
129 LET M$=CHR$(156)  : REM MAGENTA OR PURPLE
131 LET G$=CHR$(30)   : REM GREEN
133 LET C$=CHR$(159)  : REM CYAN
135 LET Y$=CHR$(158)  : REM YELLOW
```

If colours are available on your computer then put in the appropriate code numbers; otherwise delete B$, R$, etc.

WAIT

```
140 DIM A(10)
150 DIM P(6)
160 LET CAR=0.1 : REM CUSTOMER ARRIVAL RATE
170 LET CSR=0.15: REM CUSTOMER SERVICE RATE
180 LET DAY=1
190 LET PR=0 : REM PROFIT
200 REM %%%%%%%%%%%%%%%%%%%%% START OF DAY %%%%%%%%%%%%%%%%%%%%%%%%%%%%
210 PRINT CS$; : REM CLS
220 PRINT R$+"     BOUTIQUEUES"
230 PRINT B$+"       DAY ";DAY
240 PRINT
250 PRINT B$+"ARRIVAL RATE=";INT(600*CAR)/10
260 PRINT
270 PRINT M$+"$100 TO ADVERTISE?"
280 PRINT M$+"Y OR N ";
290 INPUT A$
300 LET AD=0
310 IF A$="Y" THEN LET CAR=CAR+0.1
320 IF A$="Y" THEN LET AD=1
330 PRINT
340 PRINT B$+"NEW ARRIVAL RATE=";INT(600*CAR)/10
350 PRINT
360 LET DIS=1
370 PRINT M$+"10% DISCOUNT? Y OR N"
380 INPUT A$
390 IF A$="Y" THEN LET DIS=0.9
400 IF A$="Y" THEN LET CAR=CAR+0.1
410 PRINT
420 PRINT B$+"NEW ARRIVAL RATE=";INT(600*CAR)/10
430 PRINT
440 PRINT B$+"SERVICE RATE= 9/HOUR" .
450 PRINT
460 PRINT M$+"ASSISTANTS REQUIRED"
470 PRINT M$+"AT $200? 1-10";
480 INPUT AS
490 LET AS=INT(AS+0.5)
500 IF AS<1 OR AS>10 THEN GOTO 480
510 LET MAX=2+INT(AS/4)
520 PRINT
530 PRINT B$+"MAX QUEUE LENGTH";MAX;"
540 FOR I=1 TO AS
550 LET A(I)=0
560 NEXT I
570 PRINT C$+" PRESS Y TO GO ON";
580 GET H$ : REM LET H$=INKEY$
590 IF H$<>"Y" THEN GOTO 580
600 REM %%%%%%%%%%%%%%%%%%%%% DAYS EVENTS %%%%%%%%%%%%%%%%%%%%%%%%%%%%
610 PRINT CS$ : REM CLS
620 PRINT R$+"     BOUTIQUEUES"
630 PRINT
640 PRINT R$+"DAY";DAY;" OPEN 1000-1600"
650 PRINT
660 PRINT R$+"ASSISTANTS: ";AS
670 PRINT
680 LET LC=0 : REM LOST CUSTOMERS
690 LET TT=0 : REM TOTAL TILL RECEIPTS
```

You are asked whether you want to advertise and/or give a 10% discount. You are then asked for the number of assistants.

```
700 LET Q=0 : REM LENGTH OF QUEUE
710 LET T=0 : REM TIME IN MINUTES
720 GOSUB 1710
800 REM %%%%%%%%%%%%%%%%%%%%% MINUTE BY MINUTE %%%%%%%%%%%%%%%%%%%%%
810 FOR T=1 TO 360
820 IF T>TA THEN GOSUB 1710
830 LET TS=0 : REM NUMBER OF ASSISTANTS SERVING
840 FOR J=1 TO AS
850 IF Q>0 AND A(J)<=T THEN GOSUB 1910
860 IF A(J)>T THEN LET TS=TS+1
870 NEXT J
880 LET P=7
890 GOSUB 2010
900 PRINT G$+"TIME: ";1000+T+40*INT(T/60)
910 PRINT
920 PRINT B$+"ARRIVAL RATE";STR$(INT(600*CAR)/10);"  "
930 PRINT
940 PRINT M$+"CUSTOMERS WAITING";Q
950 PRINT
960 PRINT C$+"ASSISTANTS SERVING";STR$(TS);" "
970 PRINT
980 PRINT Y$+"CUSTOMERS LOST";LC
990 PRINT
1000 PRINT R$+"TILL RECEIPTS";TT
1010 NEXT T
1100 REM %%%%%%%%%%%%%%%%%%%%% END OF DAY SUMMARY %%%%%%%%%%%%%%%%%%%%%
1110 LET P(DAY)=INT(TT-200*AS-100*AD+0.5)
1120 LET PR=PR+P(DAY)
1130 LET LC=LC+Q
1140 PRINT CS$ : REM CLS
1150 PRINT R$+"     BOUTIQUEUES"
1160 PRINT
1170 PRINT R$+"SUMMARY : DAY";DAY
1180 PRINT
1190 PRINT B$+"ARRIVAL RATE=";INT(600*CAR)/10
1200 PRINT
1210 PRINT B$+"SERVICE RATE= 9/HOUR"
1220 PRINT
1230 PRINT B$+"ASSISTANTS";AS
1240 PRINT
1250 PRINT Y$+"LOST CUSTOMERS";LC
1260 PRINT
1270 PRINT R$+"TILL RECEIPTS";TT
1280 PRINT
1290 PRINT B$+"PROFIT ";P(DAY)
1300 PRINT
1310 PRINT G$+"   PRESS Y TO GO ON"
1320 GET H$ : REM LET H$=INKEY$
1330 IF H$<>"Y" THEN GOTO 1320
1340 LET DAY=DAY+1
1350 IF DAY<7 THEN GOTO 210
1400 REM %%%%%%%%%%%%%%%%%%%%% END OF WEEK %%%%%%%%%%%%%%%%%%%%%
1410 PRINT CS$ : REM CLS
1420 PRINT R$+"     BOUTIQUEUES"
1430 PRINT
1440 PRINT B$+"    SUMMARY FOR WEEK"
```

A minute by minute account is provided.

An end of day summary is provided.

An end of week summary.

```
1450 PRINT
1460 PRINT R$+"     DAY     PROFIT"
1470 FOR I=1 TO 6
1480 PRINT "    ";I;TAB(13-LEN(STR$(P(I))));P(I)
1490 NEXT I
1500 PRINT
1510 PRINT R$+"  TOTAL";TAB(13-LEN(STR$(PR)));PR
1600 REM %%%%%%%%%%%%%%%%%%%%%%% ANOTHER WEEK? %%%%%%%%%%%%%%%%%%%%%%%%%%
1610 PRINT
1620 PRINT C$+" ANOTHER WEEK? Y OR N"+B$
1630 GET H$ : REM LET H$=INKEY$
1640 IF H$<>"Y" AND H$<>"N" THEN GOTO 1630
1650 IF H$="Y" THEN GOTO 160
1660 END : REM STOP
1700 REM %%%%%%%%%%%%%%%%%%%%% TIME OF NEXT CUSTOMER %%%%%%%%%%%%%%%%%%%%
1710 LET Q=Q+1
1720 LET TA=T-LOG(RND(1))/CAR
1730 IF Q<=MAX THEN RETURN
1740 REM %%%%%%%%% LOST CUSTOMERS %%%%%%%%%
1750 LET Q=MAX
1760 LET P=19
1770 GOSUB 2010
1780 PRINT Y$+"     LONG QUEUE"
1790 PRINT Y$+"   CUSTOMER   LOST"
1800 FOR I=1 TO 200
1810 NEXT I
1820 LET P=19
1830 GOSUB 2010
1840 PRINT "                    "
1850 PRINT "                    "
1860 LET LC=LC+1
1870 LET CAR=0.1+(CAR-0.1)*0.9
1880 RETURN
1900 REM %%%%%%%%%%%%%%%%%%%%%%% ASSISTANTS SERVING TIME %%%%%%%%%%%%%%%%%%%
1910 LET Q=Q-1
1920 LET SA=LOG(RND(1))/CSR
1930 LET A(J)=T-SA
1940 LET TT=TT-INT(SA*(1+RND(1))*DIS)
1950 RETURN

2000 REM %%%%%%%%%%%%%%%%%%%%% PRINT P LINES %%%%%%%%%%%%%%%%%%%%%%%%%%%
2005 REM PRINT AT P,0
2010 PRINT HM$;
2020 FOR I=1 TO P
2030 PRINT
2040 NEXT I
2050 RETURN
```

This calculates the time of arrival of each customer.

If the queue is too long then a message is flashed on the screen.

This calculates the time that each customer is served and the amount received from the customer.

Use PRINT AT P,0 if available.

See the Appendix for further notes.

```
            BOUTIQUEUES
              DAY  1

   ARRIVAL RATE= 6

   $100 TO ADVERTISE?
   Y OR N ? Y

   NEW ARRIVAL RATE= 12

   10% DISCOUNT? Y OR N
   ? Y

   NEW ARRIVAL RATE= 18

   SERVICE RATE= 9/HOUR

   ASSISTANTS REQUIRED
   AT $200? 1-10? 3

   MAX QUEUE LENGTH 2

     PRESS Y TO GO ON
```

```
            BOUTIQUEUES

   DAY 1   OPEN 1000-1600

   ASSISTANTS:   3

   TIME:   1421

   ARRIVAL RATE 14.7

   CUSTOMERS WAITING 2

   ASSISTANTS SERVING 3

   CUSTOMERS LOST 3

   TILL RECEIPTS 678
```

```
        BOUTIQUEUES

SUMMARY : DAY 1

ARRIVAL RATE= 14.7

SERVICE RATE= 9/HOUR

ASSISTANTS 3

LOST CUSTOMERS 3

TILL RECEIPTS 863

PROFIT   163

  PRESS Y TO GO ON
```

```
        BOUTIQUEUES

    SUMMARY FOR WEEK

    DAY     PROFIT
     1       163
     2       172
     3       370
     4       336
     5       504
     6       284

   TOTAL    1829

 ANOTHER WEEK? Y OR N
```

PRETTY PICTURES
about functions of two variables

The area of a rectangle of length 4 centimetres by 6 centimetres is simply 4*6 = 24 square centimetres. More generally, the area Z of a rectangle of length X by Y is given by the formula Z = X*Y. We say that Z is a function of X and Y, or Z is a **function of two variables** X and Y.

There are many such instances where one quantity is dependent on two other quantities. Another example is given by the formula for the volume V of a cylinder of height HT and radius R. This formula is

$$V = PI*R*R*HT$$

The value of V depends upon the values of R and HT (the value of PI does not vary). Thus V is a function of the two variables R and HT.

Here are some further examples of functions of two variables.

```
Z = COS(X*Y)
Z = COS(X*EXP(-Y/5))
Z = SIN(X)*COS(Y)
Z = COS(X)*COS(Y)
Z = X - X*X*X/12 - Y*Y/2 + 1/4
Z = 5 - (X+2)*(X+1)*(X-1)*(X-2) - Y*Y
```

What do these functions "look like"? In the second chapter we learnt how to draw graphs of functions (of one variable). Recall what we did there. If Y is a function of X, then for each value of X we calculated the corresponding value of Y and plotted a point with coordinates (X,Y).

For functions of two variables we can attempt a similar procedure. If Z is a function of X and Y then for each value of X and Y we may calculate the corresponding value of Z. If we had three dimensions at our disposal then we could plot a point at height Z above the point with coordinates (X,Y). The result would be a surface, much like a model of an island.

Our computer screen or piece of paper does not have three dimensions. We therefore have to picture these three dimensions within two dimensions; much like a photograph or drawing of a cube.

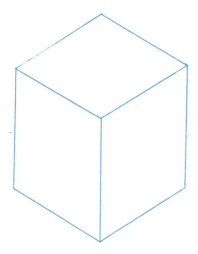

We imagine the cube as a piece of three-dimensional space in which our graph is to be drawn. We call the nearest bottom corner the origin. The bottom-right edge is the X axis and the edge on the left is the Y axis. The vertical distance represents the third dimension.

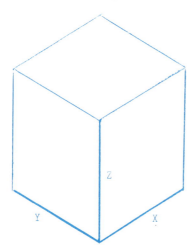

The bottom of the cube therefore represents the X-Y plane, and points there are represented by the cartesian coordinates (X,Y).

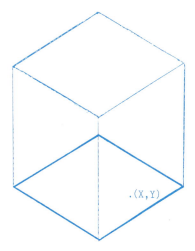

To draw our graph we look at the points (X,Y) in the base of our cube, calculate the corresponding value of Z and place a point at a distance Z above this point.

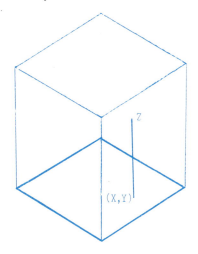

In order to do the plotting on our screen we need to know the correspondence between the coordinates on our screen and the coordinates on the cube. If (A,B) denotes the screen coordinates of a point in the base of our cube then the values of X and Y are given by the following formulae; where S has the value SQR(2)/2.

X = S*A + S*B
Y = -S*A + S*B

To do the plotting we look at the points in the base of our cube. Suppose such a point has coordinates (A,B) on our screen. The corresponding coordinates (X,Y) on the base of the cube are calculated by the formula above. Then the value of Z is calculated using the values of X and Y. We are now ready to plot a point at coordinates (A,B+Z) on our screen. However, to obtain a better perspective we reduce the vertical height by multiplying by S; we therefore plot a point at coordinates (A,S*(B+Z)) on our screen.

If we plotted a point for every point in the base of our cube then the result would be a mess. To overcome this we plot only selected points, usually the points on certain lines parallel to the X axis and/or the Y axis. This gives a cross-sectional effect. An example is given below.

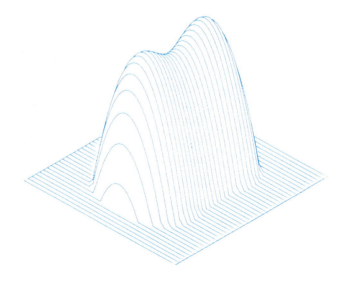

Some further examples appear on the next two pages.

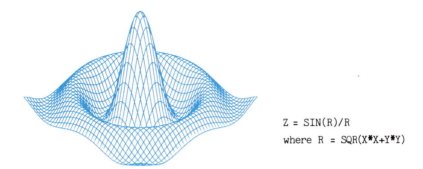

Z = SIN(R)/R
where R = SQR(X*X+Y*Y)

Z = -SIN(R)/R
where R = SQR(X*X+Y*Y)

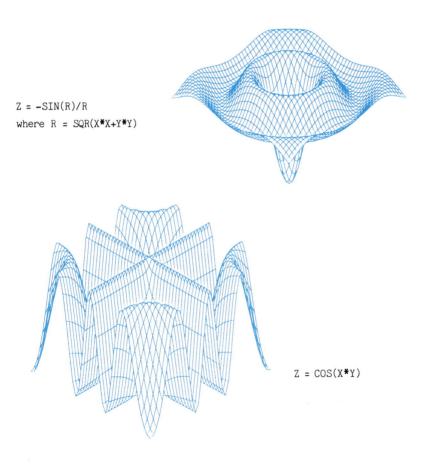

Z = COS(X*Y)

PRETTY PICTURES

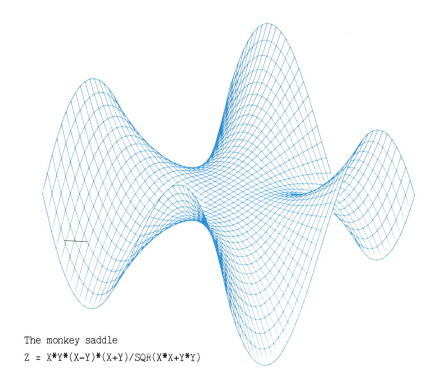

The monkey saddle
Z = X*Y*(X-Y)*(X+Y)/SQR(X*X+Y*Y)

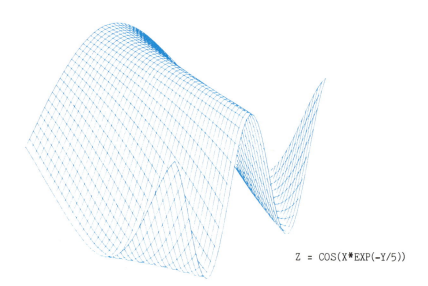

Z = COS(X*EXP(-Y/5))

PRETTY PICTURES

The program SURFACES enables you to draw graphs of functions of two variables. The quality of the resulting picture will, of course, depend upon the graphics facilities on your computer. The program contains five sample functions. You can add more if you wish.

The program has a "hidden point" algorithm; this means that points on the graph hidden by other points are not plotted.

```
10 REM                    ***********
20 REM                    *         *
30 REM                    * SURFACES *
40 REM                    *         *
50 REM                    ***********
60 REM
70 REM
100 REM %%%%%%%%%%%%%%%%%%%% SETTING UP %%%%%%%%%%%%%%%%%%%%%%%%%%%%%%
110 LET CS$=CHR$(147) : REM CODE FOR CLEAR SCREEN
120 LET SX=176 : REM SCREEN SIZE HORIZ
130 LET SY=160 : REM SCREEN SIZE VERT
140 LET RATIO=0.6 : REM TO MAKE HORIZ & VERT LINES SAME LENGTH
150 LET HY=SY/2
160 LET HX=SX/2
170 LET S=SQR(2)/2
180 LET AA=HX*S
185 GOSUB 1310 : REM EXTRA SETTINGS FOR VIC 20
190 PRINT CS$ : REM CLS
200 PRINT "     SURFACES"
210 PRINT
220 PRINT "1. Z = COS(R)"
230 PRINT
240 PRINT "2. Z = EXP(-R*R)"
250 PRINT
260 PRINT "3. Z = SIN(R)/R"
270 PRINT
280 PRINT " WHERE R=SQR(X*X+Y*Y)"
290 PRINT
300 PRINT "4. Z = COS(X)*COS(Y)"
310 PRINT
320 PRINT "5. THE MONKEY SADDLE"
330 PRINT
340 REM ROOM FOR MORE FUNCTIONS
400 PRINT "TYPE IN THE NUMBER OF"
410 PRINT "THE EQUATION";
420 INPUT N
430 PRINT CS$ : REM CLS
440 GOSUB 1010 : REM PREPARE SCREEN IF NECESSARY
500 REM %%%%%%%%%%%%%%%%%%%% PLOTTING %%%%%%%%%%%%%%%%%%%%%%%%%%%%%%
510 FOR A=-AA TO AA+5*S
520 LET MAX=-HY
530 LET BB=AA+A-10*S*INT((A+ABS(A))/(10*S))
540 FOR B=-BB TO BB+S*4 STEP 10*S
550 LET X=S*(A+B)
560 LET Y=S*(B-A)
```

Put in the correct values of SX, SY and RATIO for your computer.

Further functions may be added if desired.

Notice what happens if you RUN this program and type a number different to one of the numbers 1 to 5.

This is the main plotting routine.

```
570 LET Z=B
580 LET R=SQR(X*X+Y*Y)
590 IF N=1 THEN LET Z=10*COS(R/5)+B
600 IF N=2 THEN LET Z=75*EXP(-R*R/600)+B
610 IF N=3 AND R<>0 THEN LET Z=125*SIN(R/5)/R+B
620 IF N=4 THEN LET Z=10*COS(X/10)*COS(Y/10)+B
630 IF N=5 AND R<>0 THEN LET Z=X*Y*(X-Y)*(X+Y)/(1000*R)+B
640 REM ROOM FOR MORE FUNCTIONS
700 IF Z<MAX THEN GOTO 760
710 LET MAX=Z
720 LET U=HX+A
730 LET V=HY+Z*S/RATIO
740 IF V<0 OR V>SY THEN GOTO 760
750 GOSUB 1110 : REM PLOT U,V
760 NEXT B
770 NEXT A

800 REM %%%%%%%%%%%%%%%%%%%%%% ENDING AND ANOTHER GO %%%%%%%%%%%%%%%%%%%%%%
810 GET G$ : REM LET G$=INKEY$
820 IF G$="" THEN GOTO 810
830 GOSUB 1210 : REM RESTORE SCREEN IF NECESSARY
840 PRINT CS$ : REM CLS
850 PRINT " ANOTHER GO?  Y OR N"
860 GET G$ : REM LET G$=INKEY$
870 IF G$<>"Y" AND G$<>"N" THEN GOTO 860
880 IF G$="Y" THEN GOTO 190
890 END : REM STOP
1000 REM %%%%%%%%%%%%%%%%%%%%%% PREPARE HI-RES SCREEN FOR VIC 20 %%%%%%%%%%
1010 POKE 36869,R8+12:POKE 36867,(PEEK(36867) AND 128) OR 21
1020 FOR I=RR TO SS:POKE I,0:NEXT I
1030 FOR I=0 TO 219:POKE PP+I,I-32*Q:POKE QQ+I,2:NEXT I
1040 RETURN
1100 REM %%%%%%%%%%%%%%%%%%%%%% PLOT VIA POKE FOR VIC 20 %%%%%%%%%%%%%%%%%%
1110 V=SY-V
1120 J=INT(U/8)
1130 L=INT(U-8*J)
1140 I=INT(V/16)
1150 K=INT(V-16*I)
1160 W=RR+I*352+J*16+K
1170 POKE W,PEEK(W) OR 2↑(7-L)
1180 RETURN
1200 REM %%%%%%%%%%%%%%%%%%%%%% RESTORE SCREEN FOR VIC 20 %%%%%%%%%%%%%%%%%
1210 POKE 36869,R8:POKE 36867,R6:POKE 198,0
1220 RETURN
1300 REM %%%%%%%%%%%%%%%%%%%%%% VIC 20 SETTINGS %%%%%%%%%%%%%%%%%%%%%%%%%%%
1310 Q=PEEK(44)>=18:PP=7680+Q*3584:QQ=38400+Q*512
1320 IFQ=-1ANDPEEK(44)<32THEN PRINT "PROGRAM ABORTED - SEE APPENDIX":END
1330 RR=4096-Q*512:SS=RR+3583:R8=PEEK(36869):R6=PEEK(36867)
1340 RETURN
```

Using MAX prevents "hidden points" being plotted.

If your computer has PLOT facilities then ignore the GOSUB statements.

If you need to plot by POKEing then put in the appropriate details here.

See the Appendix for further notes.

```
      SURFACES
1. Z = COS(R)
2. Z = EXP(-R*R)
3. Z = SIN(R)/R
 WHERE R=SQR(X*X+Y*Y)
4. Z = COS(X)*COS(Y)
5. THE MONKEY SADDLE
TYPE IN THE NUMBER OF
THE EQUATION? 1
```

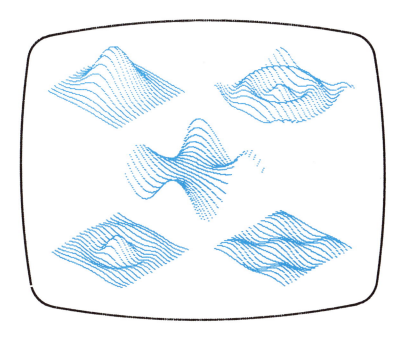

There is an alternative way of drawing pictures of functions of two variables. The idea is similar to that used in an atlas containing physical or relief maps. These maps use contours and colour to indicate the height above (or below) sea-level of the terrain. **Contours** are curves drawn through points that are of the same height above (or below) sea-level. You can get a pretty good idea of how hilly or flat a region is by looking at such a map.

In a similar way we can draw a "contour map" of a function of two variables. It provides a good idea of what the function looks like. As an example the graph of a function is shown below while the corresponding contour map is shown on the opposite page.

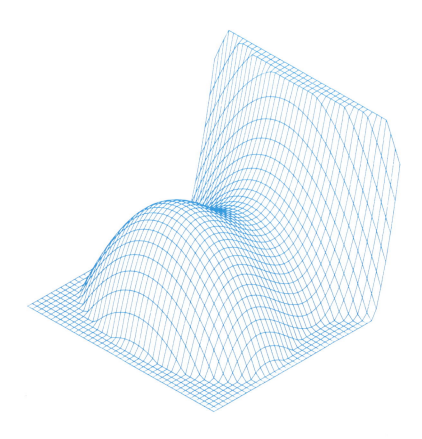

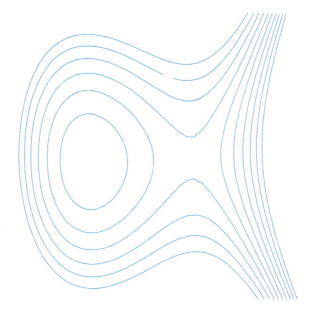

By using colour and/or various symbols we can draw contour maps on our screen. The results produce beautiful and interesting patterns. An example with the function Z = COS(X*EXP(-Y/5)) is given below.

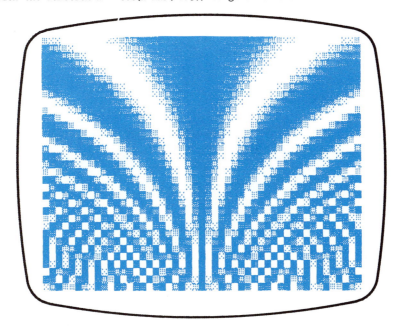

To produce contour maps we think of our screen as being the X,Y coordinates. For each point (X,Y) on the screen we calculate the value of Z. If Z is large then we place a dark "blob" at (X,Y). If Z is small we place a light one. Values of Z in between are given various shades depending on what is available on the computer.

The program CONTOURS draws relief or contour maps of fuctions of two variables.

```
10 REM                       ************
20 REM                       *          *
30 REM                       * CONTOURS *
40 REM                       *          *
50 REM                       ************
60 REM
70 REM
100 REM %%%%%%%%%%%%%%%%%%%%%% SETTING UP %%%%%%%%%%%%%%%%%%%%%%%%%%%%
110 LET C$=CHR$(147) : REM CODE FOR CLEAR SCREEN
120 LET HM$=CHR$(19) : REM CODE FOR HOME
130 LET PX=22 : REM NO. OF HORIZ PRINT POSITIONS
140 LET PY=23 : REM NO. OF VERT PRINT POSITIONS
```

PX and PY describe the screen size. Put in the values of PX and PY for your computer.

```
150 LET AX=(PX-3)/2
160 LET AY=(PY-3)/2
170 DIM C$(8)
180 LET C$(1)=CHR$(5)   : REM WHITE
190 LET C$(2)=CHR$(158) : REM YELLOW
200 LET C$(3)=CHR$(159) : REM CYAN
210 LET C$(4)=CHR$(30)  : REM MAGENTA
220 LET C$(5)=CHR$(156) : REM GREEN
230 LET C$(6)=CHR$(31)  : REM BLUE
240 LET C$(7)=CHR$(28)  : REM RED
250 LET C$(8)=CHR$(144) : REM BLACK
260 LET P$=CHR$(18)+" "+CHR$(146) : REM ■
270 REM LET P$="▓"
```

Change the order of the colours if you like.

Put in the correct colour codes for your computer. For the ZX Spectrum you will also need to change line 170 to read DIM C$(8,2). If colour is not available on your computer then some symbols will have to be chosen. Two suggestions are given below.

```
180 LET C$(1)=" "              180 LET C$(1)=" "
190 LET C$(2)=" "              190 LET C$(2)=":"
200 LET C$(3)="▒"              200 LET C$(3)="."
210 LET C$(4)="▒"              210 LET C$(4)="="
220 LET C$(5)="X"              220 LET C$(5)="+"
230 LET C$(6)="X"              230 LET C$(6)="$"
240 LET C$(7)="■"              240 LET C$(7)="X"
250 LET C$(8)="■"              250 LET C$(8)="*"
260 LET P$=""                  260 LET P$=""
```

PRETTY PICTURES

P$ represents an inverse or reverse square, that is, a solid square. If this is not available use some alternative.

```
300 REM %%%%%%%% FUNCTION CHOICE %%%%%%%%
310 PRINT CS$ : REM CLS
320 PRINT "WHICH FUNCTION DO YOU WANT? TYPE THE NUMBER"
330 PRINT
340 PRINT "1. Z=COS(X*Y)"
350 PRINT
360 PRINT "2. Z=COS(X*EXP(-Y/5))"
370 PRINT
380 PRINT "3. Z="
390 PRINT " COS(X*Y/SQR(X*X+Y*Y))"
400 PRINT "4.Z=COS(Y/(ABS(X)+.5))"
410 PRINT "5. Z=COS((X+Y)/"
420 PRINT "     (LOG(X*X+Y↑4+.5)))"
430 PRINT "6. Z=SIN((X+Y)/"
440 PRINT "     LOG(ABS(X*Y)+1.1))"
450 PRINT "7. Z=SIN(X)*COS(Y)"
460 PRINT
470 INPUT F
480 PRINT
490 PRINT "SCALE - LARGE NUMBER  GIVES LARGE RANGE"
500 PRINT "SCALE ";
510 INPUT S
600 REM %%%%%%%%%%%%%%%%%%%% PLOTTING %%%%%%%%%%%%%%%%%%%%%%%%%%
610 PRINT CS$ : REM CLS
620 FOR J=-AY TO AY
630 PRINT " ";
640 FOR I=-AX TO AX
650 LET X=I*S/2
660 LET Y=J*S/2
670 LET Z=1
680 IF F=1 THEN LET Z=COS(X*Y)
690 IF F=2 THEN LET Z=COS(X*EXP(-Y/5))
700 IF F=3 AND X*X+Y*Y<>0 THEN LET Z=COS(X*Y/SQR(X*X+Y*Y))
710 IF F=4 THEN LET Z=COS(Y/(ABS(X)+.5))
720 IF F=5 THEN LET Z=COS((X+Y)/(LOG(X*X+Y↑4+.5)))
730 IF F=6 THEN LET Z=SIN((X+Y)/LOG(ABS(X*Y)+1.1))
740 IF F=7 THEN LET Z=SIN(X)*COS(Y)
750 LET W=INT(4*Z+5)
760 IF W<1 THEN LET W=1
770 IF W>8 THEN LET W=8
780 PRINT C$(W)+P$;
790 NEXT I
800 PRINT " ";
810 NEXT J
820 PRINT HM$;C$(6); : REM PRINT AT 0,0
900 REM %%%%%%%%%%%%%%%%%%%% ENDING AND ANOTHER GO %%%%%%%%%%%%%%%%%%%%
910 GET G$ : REM LET G$=INKEY$
920 IF G$="" THEN GOTO 910
930 PRINT "  ANOTHER GO? Y OR N"
940 GET G$ : REM LET G$=INKEY$
950 IF G$<>"Y" AND G$<>"N" THEN GOTO 940
960 IF G$="Y" THEN GOTO 310
970 PRINT CS$ : REM CLS
```

Seven different functions are included.

The value of S determines the ranges of X and Y over which the plotting is done. Try the values 10, 1, 0.1, etc.

This is the main plotting routine.

The program will wait until some key is pressed before continuing.

```
WHICH FUNCTION DO YOU
WANT? TYPE THE NUMBER

1. Z=COS(X*Y)

2. Z=COS(X*EXP(-Y/5))

3. Z=
   COS(X*Y/SQR(X*X+Y*Y))

4. Z=COS(Y/(ABS(X)+.5))

5. Z=COS((X+Y)/
       (LOG(X*X+Y↑4+.5)))

6. Z=SIN((X+Y)/
       LOG(ABS(X*Y)+1.1))

7. Z=SIN(X)*COS(Y)

? 1
SCALE - LARGE NUMBER
GIVES LARGE RANGE
SCALE ? 1
```

PRETTY PICTURES

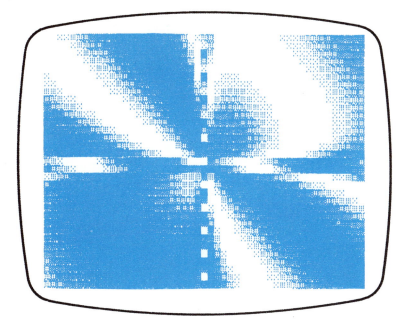

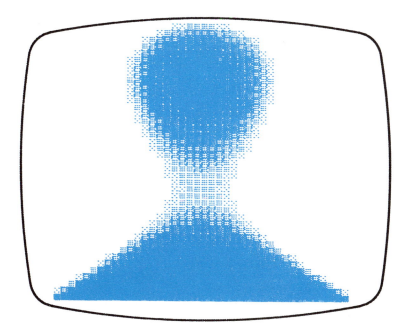

PRETTY PICTURES

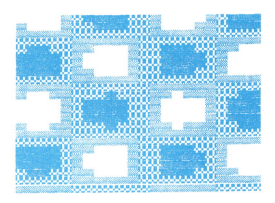

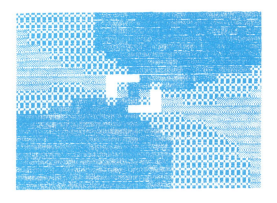

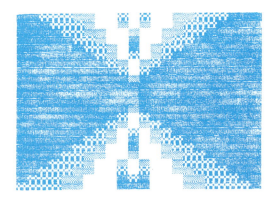

ON THE MOVE
about differential equations

We have all dropped a stone into a well to find out how deep it is. The equation which tells you (albeit roughly) the distance S that the stone falls after T seconds is $S = G*T^2/2$. Here G is a constant that takes the value 32 if we are working in feet and 9.8 if we are working in metres (it is the acceleration due to gravity). Thus, for example, after 2 seconds the stone will fall $32*2*2/2 = 64$ feet if unimpeded.

In many physical situations the equation that we obtain involves the rate of change of one variable. Indeed in the example just discussed it is the rate of change of distance that is directly proportional to time. This relationship can be expressed as

$$\frac{dS}{dT} = G*T$$

or else as

$$S' = G*T$$

where the left-hand side of the above equations represent "the rate of change of S with respect to T" (in this case it is the velocity or speed of the stone).

If you are familiar with calculus (do not worry if you are not) then you will see how each of the following equations can be obtained from the other.

$$S = G*T^2/2$$

$$S' = G*T \quad \text{(with S=0 if T=0)}$$

The second equation is called a **differential equation** and the conditions within the brackets are called the initial conditions. The first equation is called the **solution** of the differential equation. It is so called because the rate of change of $G*T^2/2$ is precisely $G*T$. A related example is the following one, where V stands for velocity.

$$V = G*T$$

$$V' = G \quad \text{(with } V=\emptyset \text{ if } T=\emptyset\text{)}$$

Here the second equation is a differential equation with the first being its solution. In words this differential equation states that the rate of change of velocity is constant, that is, the acceleration of the object is constant.

Courses on differential equations usually concentrate on differential equations whose solutions can be expressed in terms of explicit mathematical formulae. However, in practice most differential equations are too complicated to solve in this manner. For example, look at the following equation.

$$Y' = 1 - Y + K*Y^3*SIN(T)$$

Now no formula for Y in terms of T can be found if $K \neq \emptyset$, although a formula exists when $K = \emptyset$. This does not mean that a solution does not exist, it just means that an explicit mathematical formula cannot be found. However approximations can be found by using computers. These provide numerical solutions, and often this is all that we require.

Let us return to the falling stone example again. Let V_N denote the velocity after N seconds. The differential equation tells us that the rate of change of velocity is G. Thus each second we expect the velocity to change by G. We therefore get the equation below.

$$V_{N+1} = V_N + G$$

Given a value of $V_\emptyset$ we may use this equation, repeatedly, to determine a value of V_N, for any value of N.

What about the distance S? In one second the distance covered is equal to the average velocity. Look at the time interval from N-1 to N seconds. Since the acceleration is constant, the average velocity is the same as the velocity at half-time, at time N - 1/2 seconds. Since the velocity changes by G each second it changes by G/2 in 1/2 second. Thus the average velocity is given by V_{N-1} + G/2, which is the same as V_N - G/2. Let S_N

denote the distance that the object falls after N seconds. Then S_N will equal the distance covered during the first N-1 seconds plus the distance covered during the next second. This gives us the equation below.

$$S_N = S_{N-1} + V_N - G/2$$

Your microcomputer can use such equations, iteratively in a loop, to calculate the velocity and distance of a falling stone.

The program FALLING STONE illustrates the ideas mentioned above by calculating the velocity and distance of a falling stone during a 10 second interval.

```
10 REM                   *****************
20 REM                   *               *
30 REM                   * FALLING STONE *
40 REM                   *               *
50 REM                   *****************
60 REM
70 REM
100 PRINT CHR$(147) : REM CLEAR SCREEN
110 PRINT "    FALLING STONE"
120 PRINT
130 LET V=0 : REM INITIAL VELOCITY
140 LET S=0 : REM INITIAL DISTANCE
150 PRINT "TIME  VEL.  DIST."
160 PRINT
170 FOR T=0 TO 10
180 PRINT TAB(3-LEN(STR$(T)));T;
190 PRINT TAB(9-LEN(STR$(V)));V;
200 PRINT TAB(16-LEN(STR$(S)));S
210 LET V=V+32
220 LET S=S+V-16
230 NEXT T
```

See the Appendix for some general notes.

What happens if you interchange lines 210 and 220 in FALLING STONE?

```
          FALLING STONE
  TIME    VEL.    DIST.
    0       0        0
    1      32       16
    2      64       64
    3      96      144
    4     128      256
    5     160      400
    6     192      576
    7     224      784
    8     256     1024
    9     288     1296
   10     320     1600
```

This method of solving differential equations is called the **Euler-Cauchy** method, although strictly speaking we have used the **modified Euler-Cauchy** method for the problem involving distance. In general the Euler-Cauchy method gives an approximate solution to differential equations, although in the FALLING STONE example above it provides an accurate one. Leonard Euler (1707-1783) was a Swiss mathematician who made numerous contributions to many branches of mathematics. He studied nearly every area of mathematics and published about 1000 papers. Baron Augustin-Louis Cauchy (1789-1857) was a French mathematician who was also very prolific, perhaps the most prolific mathematician; he sometimes published a paper a day. He developed the rigorous treatment of calculus by providing the so-called "delta-epsilon" approach.

The next program BOUNCING BALL extends the ideas just discussed a little further. A ball is thrown from the top left-hand corner of the screen and falls to the bottom, bouncing off the sides and the bottom. Each time the ball bounces off a side it loses 80% of its speed, each time it bounces off the bottom it loses 70% of its speed. Thus eventually the ball will stop. You INPUT the initial (horizontal) velocity VH. The vertical velocity VV is determined as in the FALLING STONE program. As an added feature you can have the path (track) of the ball displayed on your screen. Notice the shape of this track.

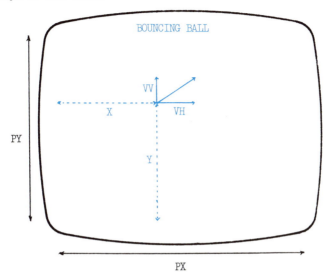

The diagram above illustrates the meaning of the variables in the program BOUNCING BALL.

```
10 REM                    ******************
20 REM                    *                *
30 REM                    * BOUNCING BALL  *
40 REM                    *                *
50 REM                    ******************
60 REM
70 REM
100 REM ////////////////////// SETTING UP //////////////////////////////
110 LET P=8164+(PEEK(44))>=18)*3584 : REM START OF POKE
120 POKE 36879,170 : REM SCREEN COLOUR
130 LET CS$=CHR$(147) : REM CODE FOR CLEAR SCREEN
140 LET HM$=CHR$(19) : REM CODE FOR HOME
150 LET PX=22 : REM NO. OF HORIZ PRINT POSITIONS
160 LET PY=23 : REM NO. OF VERT PRINT POSITIONS
170 LET PX=PX-1
180 LET PY=PY-1
190 LET H=0.1
```

PX and PY denote the number of PRINT, PLOT or POKE positions. A low resolution is good, otherwise the program runs a bit too slowly.

The factor H controls the speed of display. To speed things up use a larger value of H.

```
200 REM %%%%%%%% INITIAL POSITION OF BALL %%%%%%%%%%%%%%%%%%%%%%%%%%%%
210 LET X=0
220 LET Y=PY
230 LET U=0
240 LET V=PY
250 LET VV=0
260 LET N=0
300 REM %%%%%%%%%%%%%%%%%%%%% INPUT DATA %%%%%%%%%%%%%%%%%%%%%%%%%%%%%
310 PRINT CS$ : REM CLS
320 PRINT "    BOUNCING BALL"
330 PRINT
340 PRINT "INITIAL VELOCITY OF"
350 PRINT "BALL ";
360 INPUT VH
370 PRINT
380 LET T=0
390 PRINT "DO YOU WANT A TRAIL,"
400 PRINT "Y OR N ";
410 INPUT D$
420 IF D$="Y" THEN LET T=1
430 PRINT CS$; : REM CLS
440 PRINT "    BOUNCING BALL"
500 REM %%%%%%%%%%%%%%%%%%%% CALCULATION LOOP %%%%%%%%%%%%%%%%%%%%%%%%
510 LET X=X+VH*H
520 LET VV=VV+32*H
530 LET Y=Y-VV*H+16*H*H
540 IF Y<=0 THEN GOSUB 710
550 IF X>=PX THEN GOSUB 810
560 IF X<=0 THEN GOSUB 910
570 IF T=0 THEN GOSUB 1110 : REM UNPLOT U,V
580 GOSUB 1310 : REM SOUND OFF
590 LET U=INT(X)
600 LET V=INT(Y)
610 GOSUB 1010 : REM PLOT U,V
620 IF N<16 THEN GOTO 510
630 PRINT HM$; : REM PRINT AT 0,0
640 PRINT " ANOTHER GO? Y OR N"
650 GET G$ : REM LET G$=INKEY$
660 IF G$<>"Y" AND G$<>"N" THEN GOTO 650
670 IF G$="Y" THEN GOTO 210
680 END : REM STOP
700 REM %%%%%%%%%%%%%%%%%%%%% GROUND BOUNCE %%%%%%%%%%%%%%%%%%%%%%%%%%
710 LET Y=0
720 LET VV=-0.7*VV
730 LET N=N+1
740 GOSUB 1210 : REM SOUND ON
750 RETURN
800 REM %%%%%%%%%%%%%%%%%%%%% RIGHT BOUNCE %%%%%%%%%%%%%%%%%%%%%%%%%%%
810 LET X=PX
820 LET VH=-0.8*VH
830 GOSUB 1210 : REM SOUND ON
840 RETURN
900 REM %%%%%%%%%%%%%%%%%%%%% LEFT BOUNCE %%%%%%%%%%%%%%%%%%%%%%%%%%%%
910 LET X=0
920 LET VH=-0.8*VH
930 GOSUB 1210 : REM SOUND ON
940 RETURN
```

```
1000 REM %%%%%%%%%%%%%%%%%%%%% PLOT VIA POKE %%%%%%%%%%%%%%%%%%%%%%%%%%%
1010 POKE P+U-22*V,42
1020 RETURN
1100 REM %%%%%%%%%%%%%%%%%%%%% UNPLOT VIA POKE %%%%%%%%%%%%%%%%%%%%%%%%%
1110 POKE P+U-22*V,32
1120 RETURN
1200 REM %%%%%%%%%%%%%%%%%%%%% SOUND ON %%%%%%%%%%%%%%%%%%%%%%%%%%%%%%%%
1210 POKE 36878,15                    Put your own sound effects here
1215 POKE 36876,215
1220 RETURN                           if available.
1300 REM %%%%%%%%%%%%%%%%%%%%% SOUND OFF %%%%%%%%%%%%%%%%%%%%%%%%%%%%%%%
1310 POKE 36876,0
1315 POKE 36878,0
1320 RETURN
```

```
            BOUNCING BALL

         INITIAL VELOCITY OF
         BALL? 7

         DO YOU WANT A TRAIL,
         Y OR N? Y
```

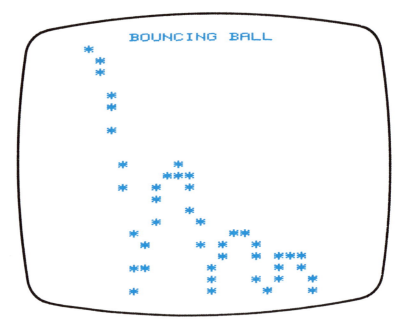

Low resolution printout.

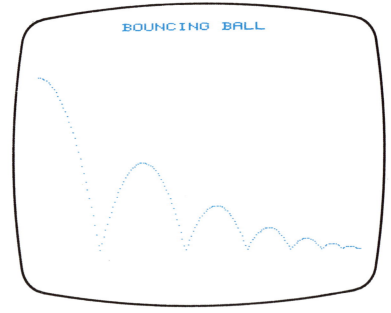

High resolution printout.

ON THE MOVE

In the real world air resistance slows down a falling or moving object. The effect that air resistance has is approximately proportional to the velocity of the moving object. Thus if we wish to include air resistance then our equation of motion becomes

$$V' = G - K*V$$

where K is some constant. The velocity at time N is the velocity at time N-1 plus the expected change in velocity (V') at time N-1. Thus the Euler-Cauchy method then leads to the following formula.

$$V_N = V_{N-1} + G - K*V_{N-1}$$

For games purposes this is usually a sufficiently good approximation.

We may use similar equations for a moving object (a car or rocket) powered by some internal force (engine). To do this we replace G by TH, the acceleration or thrust of the object. The acceleration can usually be varied by some control (accelerator or gas pedal). The equation above then changes to the one below.

$$V_N = V_{N-1} + TH - K*V_{N-1}$$

Notice that once the speed of TH/K is reached then it does not change. In particular, if the object was travelling faster than TH/K then it would slow down. Thus altering the value of TH changes the speed.

These ideas have been incorporated in a simple game FLIGHT which simulates a rocket powered aeroplane taking off and landing. You have control over the angle upwards (or downwards) that you point the aeroplane. Also you have a throttle/brake control which changes the value of TH and consequently alters your speed. You must reach a height of 500 or more before descending. If you reach ground level with vertical velocity greater than -10 then the automatic brakes will come on and you land safely. Otherwise you crash. You also crash if your horizontal velocity becomes negative.

The speeds in FLIGHT are given in metres per second. Multiplying the speeds by 2.2 converts them into miles per hour.

The equations used in FLIGHT are slightly more complicated then the ones mentioned above. We have also included some resistance which is proportional to the square of the velocity.

If you have not observed how an aeroplane lands then you may be surprised what FLIGHT will teach you.

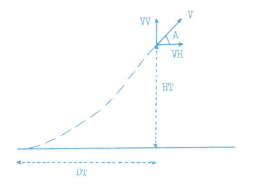

FLIGHT velocities and distances   FLIGHT forces

```
10 REM                      **********
20 REM                      *        *
30 REM                      * FLIGHT *
40 REM                      *        *
50 REM                      **********
60 REM
70 REM
100 REM %%%%%%%%%%%%%%%%%%%% SETTING UP %%%%%%%%%%%%%%%%%%%%%%%%%%
110 LET C$=CHR$(147) : REM CODE FOR CLEAR SCREEN
120 LET HM$=CHR$(19) : REM CODE FOR HOME
130 LET B$=CHR$(31) : REM BLUE
140 LET R$=CHR$(28) : REM RED
150 LET M$=CHR$(156) : REM MAGENTA OR PURPLE
160 LET G$=CHR$(30) : REM GREEN
170 LET C$=CHR$(159) : REM CYAN
180 LET Y$=CHR$(158) : REM YELLOW
```

If colours are available on your computer then put in the appropriate code numbers; otherwise delete B$, R$, etc.

```
190 LET VV=0 : REM VERTICAL VELOCITY IN METRES/SEC
200 LET VH=0.01 : REM HORIZ VELOCITY IN METRES/SEC
210 LET HT=0.01 : REM HEIGHT IN METRES
220 LET DT=0 : REM DISTANCE IN KILOMETRES
230 LET A=0 : REM ANGLE OF INCLINATION IN DEGREES
240 LET TH=0 : REM THRUST
250 LET L=0 : REM MINIMUM HEIGHT NOT REACHED
260 LET SW=0 : REM ENGINE NOT ENGAGED
300 REM %%%%%%%%%%%%%%%%%%%% INITIAL DISPLAY %%%%%%%%%%%%%%%%%%%%
310 PRINT C$ : REM CLS
320 PRINT
330 PRINT R$+"WHEN READY TO ENGAGE"
340 PRINT R$+"    ENGINE - PRESS Y"
```

```
350 GOTO 400
360 PRINT CS$ : REM CLS
370 PRINT
380 LET SW=1
390 PRINT B$+"      WE'RE OFF"
400 PRINT HM$ : REM PRINT AT 0,0
410 FOR I=1 TO 17
420 PRINT
430 NEXT I
440 PRINT B$+"CONTROLS"
450 PRINT G$+"THRUST    Z:-    C:+"
460 PRINT B$+"ANGLE     B:-    M:+"
470 GOSUB 1210
500 REM %%%%%%%%%%%%%%%%%%%%% CONTROLS %%%%%%%%%%%%%%%%%%%%%%%%%%%%%%
510 GET H$ : REM LET H$=INKEY$
520 IF H$="Z" THEN LET TH=TH-1
530 IF H$="C" THEN LET TH=TH+1
540 IF TH>15 THEN LET TH=15
550 IF H$="B" THEN LET A=A-1
560 IF H$="M" THEN LET A=A+1
570 IF H$="Y" THEN GOTO 360
580 IF SW=0 THEN GOTO 470
600 REM %%%%%%%%%%%%%%%%%%%%% CALCULATING %%%%%%%%%%%%%%%%%%%%%%%%%%
610 LET XX=COS(π*A/180)*TH-(1+VH/200)*VH/200
620 LET YY=-9.8+SIN(π*A/180)*TH-(1+VV/100)*VV/100+(6-VH/100)*VH/100
630 LET VH=INT((VH+XX)*100)/100
640 LET VV=INT((VV+YY)*100)/100
650 LET HT=INT((HT+VV-YY/2)*100)/100
660 IF L=0 AND HT>499 THEN GOSUB 1410
670 IF HT<0 THEN LET HT=0
680 IF HT=0 AND VV>-10 THEN LET VV=0
690 IF HT=0 AND VV=0 AND L=1 THEN GOTO 910
700 LET DT=INT((1000*DT+VH-XX/2))/1000
710 GOSUB 1210
720 IF HT=0 AND VV<=-10 THEN GOTO 810
730 IF VH<=0 THEN GOTO 810
740 GOTO 510
800 REM %%%%%%%%%%%%%%%%%%%%% CRASH %%%%%%%%%%%%%%%%%%%%%%%%%%%%%%%%
810 PRINT CS$ : REM CLS
820 PRINT
830 PRINT R$+"        CRASH"
840 GOSUB 1210
850 REM PUT SOUND EFFECTS HERE
851 POKE 36877,220
852 FOR I=15 TO 0 STEP -1
853 POKE 36878,I
854 FOR J=1 TO 200:NEXT J
855 NEXT I
856 POKE 36877,0
860 GOTO 1110
900 REM %%%%%%%%%%%%%%%%%%%%% SAFE LANDING %%%%%%%%%%%%%%%%%%%%%%%%%
910 PRINT CS$ : REM CLS
920 LET TH=0
930 LET A=0
940 LET VV=0
950 LET VH=0
```

You can adjust the thrust and angle before taking off. Press Y to take off.

You might like to delete line 680 and change line 690 so that

$$VV>-10$$

See what effect this has on the program.

Put your own sound effects here if available.

```
960 PRINT
970 PRINT G$+"      SAFE LANDING"
980 PRINT R$+"      WELL  DONE"
990 GOSUB 1210
1000 FOR J=1 TO 3
1010 GOSUB 1510 : REM SOUND EFFECTS
1020 NEXT J
1100 REM ZZZZZZZZZZZZZZZZZZZZZ ANOTHER GO? ZZZZZZZZZZZZZZZZZZZZZZZZZZZZZ
1110 GET H$ : REM LET H$=INKEY$
1120 IF H$<>"" THEN GOTO 1110
1130 PRINT
1140 PRINT B$+" ANOTHER GO? Y OR N"
1150 GET H$ : REM LET H$=INKEY$
1160 IF H$<>"Y" AND H$<>"N" THEN GOTO 1150
1170 IF H$="Y" THEN GOTO 190
1180 END : REM STOP
1200 REM ZZZZZZZZZZZZZZZZZZZZZ DISPLAY ZZZZZZZZZZZZZZZZZZZZZZZZZZZZZZZZZ
1210 PRINT HM$; : REM PRINT AT 0,0
1220 PRINT R$+"        FLIGHT"
1230 PRINT
1240 PRINT
1250 PRINT
1260 PRINT
1270 PRINT M$+"VERT.VEL=";STR$(VV);"    "
1280 PRINT
1290 PRINT R$+"HEIGHT=";STR$(HT);"      "
1300 PRINT
1310 PRINT G$+"THRUST=";STR$(TH);" "
1320 PRINT
1330 PRINT B$+"ANGLE=";STR$(A);" "
1340 PRINT
1350 PRINT G$+"HORIZ.VEL=";STR$(VH);"    "
1360 PRINT
1370 PRINT Y$+"DISTANCE=";STR$(DT);"   "
1380 RETURN
1400 REM ZZZZZZZZZZZZZZZZZZZZZ REACHED HEIGHT OF 500? ZZZZZZZZZZZZZZZZZZ
1410 LET L=1
1420 PRINT HM$ : REM PRINT AT 0,0
1430 PRINT
1440 PRINT R$+"     PLEASE LAND"
1450 GOSUB 1510 : REM SOUND EFFECTS
1460 RETURN
1500 REM ZZZZZZZZZZZZZZZZZZZZZ SOUND EFFECTS ZZZZZZZZZZZZZZZZZZZZZZZZZZZ
1510 POKE 36878,15
1520 POKE 36876,200
1530 FOR I=1 TO 100
1540 NEXT I
1550 POKE 36876,0
1560 POKE 36878,0
1570 FOR I=1 TO 100
1580 NEXT I
1590 RETURN
```

Under the right conditions the automatic brakes come on and you land safely.

You must reach a height of 500 before attempting to land.

Put your own sound effects here if available.

See the Appendix for further notes.

```
            FLIGHT
WHEN READY TO ENGAGE
    ENGINE - PRESS Y

VERT.VEL= 0

HEIGHT= .01

THRUST= 12

ANGLE= 14

HORIZ.VEL= .01

DISTANCE= 0


CONTROLS
THRUST    Z:-   C:+
ANGLE     B:-   M:+
```

```
            FLIGHT
         WE'RE OFF

VERT.VEL= 45.86

HEIGHT= 482.96

THRUST= 15

ANGLE= 9

HORIZ.VEL= 344.8

DISTANCE= 5.063


CONTROLS
THRUST    Z:-   C:+
ANGLE     B:-   M:+
```

```
         FLIGHT
      PLEASE LAND

  VERT.VEL=-9.21

  HEIGHT= 253.3

  THRUST= 5

  ANGLE= 13

  HORIZ.VEL= 346.93

  DISTANCE= 79.586


  CONTROLS
  THRUST     Z:-   C:+
  ANGLE      B:-   M:+
```

```
         FLIGHT

       SAFE LANDING
         WELL  DONE

  VERT.VEL= 0

  HEIGHT= 0

  THRUST= 0

  ANGLE= 0

  HORIZ.VEL= 0

  DISTANCE= 89.334


  CONTROLS
  THRUST     Z:-   C:+
  ANGLE      B:-   M:+
```

There are many additions and improvements that could be made to FLIGHT. After playing the game a few times add your own personal touch to the program. One suggestion is to take fuel into account. The additional lines required for this are given below.

```
270 LET FUEL=3000
280 REM 3000 IS EASY, 2000 IS MEDIUM, 1000 IS QUITE HARD
732 LET FUEL=FUEL-ABS(TH)
734 IF FUEL<0 THEN LET FUEL=0
736 IF FUEL=0 THEN LET TH=0
738 IF FUEL=0 THEN GOTO 610
1372 PRINT
1374 PRINT "FUEL=";STR$(FUEL);"    "
```

If we fire a rocket vertically from the Earth then there are several other factors that need to be taken into account. For example, G, the acceleration due to gravity, changes the higher up we go. Indeed this value is approximately $G0/(1+HT/R)^2$, where G0 is the value at the Earth's surface, R is the radius of the Earth and HT is the height above the Earth's surface. It is convenient to let G1 = R*R*G0 and DT = R + HT. Then the value of G is G1/(DT*DT). For small values of HT the value of DT is approximately R and so the value of G is approximately G0.

Another factor that could affect the rocket is that there is less air the higher up we go. Consequently the air resistance will change. However, the next program does not include this refinement.

In the program ORBIT a rocket or flying saucer is fired from the surface of the Earth. You have two controls at your disposal. These are called the up-thrust and the side-thrust. The up-thrust is a force directed directly away from (or towards) the centre of the Earth. This causes the rocket to go up and down. The side-thrust is a force perpendicular to the up-thrust. You use this to go "sidewards".

On RUNning ORBIT use the up-thrust and side-thrust to get your rocket into an orbit around the Earth. You have a limited (but generous) amount of fuel, so be careful with the thrust controls. If, when you run out of fuel, your velocity and height are not "just right" then you will either zoom off into outer space or else return to Earth with a big crash. It pays to keep some fuel in reserve. Also, do not go too high otherwise it will take you a long time to orbit the Earth.

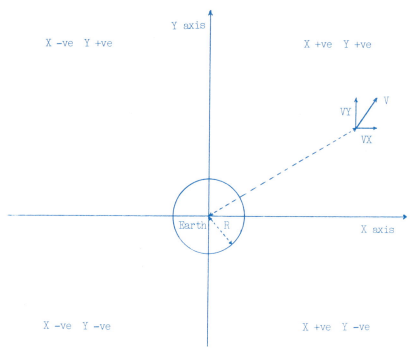

ORBIT distances and velocities

Centre of the Earth ·

ORBIT forces.

```
 10 REM                    *********
 20 REM                    *       *
 30 REM                    * ORBIT *
 40 REM                    *       *
 50 REM                    *********
 60 REM
 70 REM
100 REM %%%%%%%%%%%%%%%%%%%%% SETTING UP %%%%%%%%%%%%%%%%%%%%%%%%%%%%%
110 LET CS$=CHR$(147) : REM CODE FOR CLEAR SCREEN
120 LET HM$=CHR$(19)  : REM CODE FOR HOME
130 LET B$=CHR$(31)   : REM BLUE
132 LET R$=CHR$(28)   : REM RED
134 LET M$=CHR$(156)  : REM MAGENTA OR PURPLE
136 LET G$=CHR$(30)   : REM GREEN
138 LET C$=CHR$(159)  : REM CYAN
```

If colours are available on your computer then put in the appropriate code numbers; otherwise delete B$, R$, etc.

```
140 LET VX=0  : REM X VELOCITY IN KILOMETRES/SEC
150 LET VY=0  : REM Y VELOCITY IN KILOMETRES/SEC
160 LET V=0   : REM VELOCITY IN KILOMETRES/MIN
170 LET HT=0.1 : REM HEIGHT IN KILOMETRES
180 LET TH=0  : REM UPWARD THRUST
190 LET TS=0  : REM SIDEWARD THRUST
200 LET SW=0  : REM ENGINE NOT ENGAGED
210 LET R=6371 : REM RADIUS OF EARTH
220 LET DT=R+HT : REM DISTANCE FROM CENTRE OF EARTH
230 LET X=R+HT
240 LET Y=0
250 LET X$=STR$(X)
260 LET Y$=STR$(Y)
270 LET G1=R*R*9.81/1000 : REM A CONSTANT FOR GRAVITY
280 LET G=G1/(DT*DT)
290 LET FUEL=10000
300 REM %%%%%%%%%%%%%%%%%%%% INITIAL DISPLAY %%%%%%%%%%%%%%%%%%%%%%%%
310 PRINT CS$ : REM CLS
320 PRINT
330 PRINT R$+"WHEN READY TO ENGAGE"
340 PRINT R$+"    ENGINE - PRESS Y"
350 GOTO 400
360 PRINT CS$ : REM CLS
370 PRINT
380 LET SW=1
390 PRINT B$+"     WE'RE OFF"
400 PRINT HM$ : REM PRINT AT 0,0
410 FOR I=1 TO 18
420 PRINT
430 NEXT I
440 PRINT B$+"CONTROLS"
450 PRINT G$+"  UP-THRUST Z:-  C:+"
460 PRINT B$+"SIDE-THRUST B:-  M:+"
470 GOSUB 1010
```

Set your thrust controls before taking off.

```
500 REM %%%%%%%%%%%%%%%%%%% CONTROLS %%%%%%%%%%%%%%%%%%%%%%%%%%
510 GET H$ : REM LET H$=INKEY$
520 IF H$="Z" THEN LET TH=TH-5
530 IF H$="C" THEN LET TH=TH+5
540 IF H$="B" THEN LET TS=TS-5
550 IF H$="M" THEN LET TS=TS+5
560 IF H$="Y" THEN GOTO 360
570 IF SW=0 THEN GOTO 470
600 REM %%%%%%%%%%%%%%%%%%% CALCULATING %%%%%%%%%%%%%%%%%%%%%%
610 LET FUEL=FUEL-ABS(TH)-ABS(TS)
620 IF FUEL<=0 THEN LET TS=0
630 IF FUEL<=0 THEN LET TH=0
640 IF FUEL<0 THEN LET FUEL=0
650 LET XX=(TH/1000-G)*X/DT+TS/1000*Y/DT
660 LET YY=(TH/1000-G)*Y/DT+TS/1000*X/DT
670 LET VX=VX+XX
680 LET VY=VY+YY
690 LET V=INT(SQR(VX*VX+VY*VY)*60)
700 LET X=X+VX-XX/2
710 LET X$=STR$(INT(X*10)/10)
720 LET Y=Y+VY-YY/2
730 LET Y$=STR$(INT(Y*10)/10)
740 LET DT=SQR(X*X+Y*Y)
750 LET HT=INT((DT-R)*10)/10
760 LET G=G1/(DT*DT)
770 GOSUB 1010
780 IF FUEL=0 AND HT>=0 THEN GOTO 650
790 IF HT>=0 THEN GOTO 510
800 REM %%%%%%%%%%%%%%%%%%% CRASH %%%%%%%%%%%%%%%%%%%%%%%%%%%%
810 PRINT CS$ : REM CLS
820 PRINT
830 PRINT R$+"        CRASH"
840 GOSUB 1010
850 REM PUT SOUND EFFECTS HERE
851 POKE 36877,220
852 FOR I=15 TO 0 STEP -1
853 POKE 36878,I
854 FOR J=1 TO 200:NEXT J
855 NEXT I
856 POKE 36877,0
900 REM %%%%%%%%%%%%%%%%%%% ANOTHER GO? %%%%%%%%%%%%%%%%%%%%%%
910 GET H$ : REM LET H$=INKEY$
920 IF H$<>"" THEN GOTO 910
930 PRINT
940 PRINT B$+" ANOTHER GO? Y OR N"
950 GET H$ : REM LET H$=INKEY$
960 IF H$<>"Y" AND H$<>"N" THEN GOTO 950
970 IF H$="Y" THEN GOTO 140
980 END : REM STOP
1000 REM %%%%%%%%%%%%%%%%%% DISPLAY %%%%%%%%%%%%%%%%%%%%%%%%%%
1010 PRINT HM$; : REM PRINT AT 0,0
1020 PRINT R$+"        ORBIT"
1030 PRINT
1040 PRINT
```

Put your own sound effects here if available.

```
1050 PRINT
1060 PRINT
1070 PRINT G$+"UP THRUST=";STR$(TH);"    "
1080 PRINT
1090 PRINT B$+"SIDE THRUST=";STR$(TS);"    "
1100 PRINT
1110 PRINT M$+"HEIGHT=";STR$(HT);"  "
1120 PRINT
1130 PRINT C$+"VELOCITY=";STR$(V);" "
1140 PRINT
1150 PRINT R$+"X= ";X$;"   "
1160 PRINT
1170 PRINT R$+"Y= ";Y$;"   "
1180 PRINT
1190 PRINT M$+"FUEL= ";STR$(FUEL);"   "
1200 RETURN
```

See the Appendix for further notes.

```
                ORBIT

        WHEN READY TO ENGAGE
            ENGINE - PRESS Y

        UP-THRUST= 45

        SIDE-THRUST= 5

        HEIGHT= .1

        VELOCITY= 0

        X=   6371.1

        Y=   0

        FUEL=   10000

        CONTROLS
          UP-THRUST   Z:-   C:+
          SIDE-THRUST B:-   M:+
```

```
          ORBIT
        WE'RE OFF

UP-THRUST= 0

SIDE-THRUST= 0

HEIGHT= 1318.9

VELOCITY= 868

X= -4216.9

Y= -6430.8

FUEL=  0

CONTROLS
   UP-THRUST  Z:-   C:+
   SIDE-THRUST B:-  M:+
```

```
          ORBIT
         CRASH

UP-THRUST= 0

SIDE-THRUST= 0

HEIGHT=-2.9

VELOCITY= 1882

X=  3243.1

Y= -5480.5

FUEL=  0

   ANOTHER GO? Y OR N
```

Many additions and improvements can be made to ORBIT. For example, you could produce a visual display of the position of the rocket (see the diagrams below). Air resistance, etc. has been ignored, you may like to include this. You could also include a landing procedure.

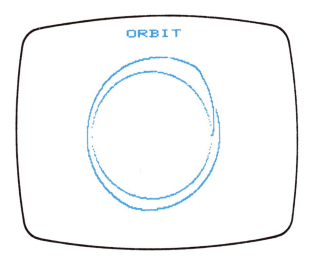

A successful orbit

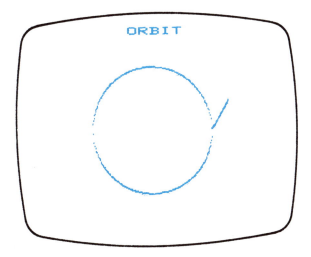

Escape into outer space

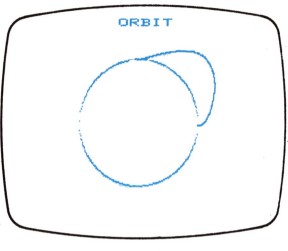

Crash

GETTING BIGGER ALL THE TIME
more on differential equations

In the previous chapter we looked at some differential equations. A very common differential equation that arises in nature is one in which the rate of growth of a quantity is proportional to the quantity itself. For example, the rate of growth of a colony of bacteria.

A living cell grows until at some stage it divides into two cells. These "daughter" cells then grow until they divide, and so the process continues. The time between two splittings is called the generation time. Not all cells in a colony divide at the same time nor does each member have the same generation time. However because the number of organisms in a colony is usually large the average generation time is relatively constant, and can be measured by observation. The rate of growth of the colony satisfies a differential equation of the following form.

$$Y' = A*Y$$

Here Y denotes the number in the colony, Y' denotes the rate of change of this number and A is a number depending on the average generation time.

The differential equation can be interpreted as saying that the number of births at any instant is proportional to the number of bacteria. Thus if there are Y_{OLD} bacteria at some given time then the number of births in a (small) unit of time is $A*Y_{OLD}$. Hence if Y_{NEW} denotes the number of bacteria one unit of time later then

$$Y_{NEW} = Y_{OLD} + A*Y_{OLD}$$

This, as you may recognise, is the Euler-Cauchy method of solving differential equations.

We can use the relation above, in a loop, to calculate the size of a colony of bacteria at time T. The following illustrates what is to be done.

```
INPUT A
INPUT T    (The time interval)
INPUT Y    (The initial number in the colony)
FOR I=1 TO T
LET Y=Y+A*Y
NEXT I
PRINT Y
```

As an example, suppose we have a colony of bacteria which grows according to the differential equation

Y' = 0.00009627*Y

where the time interval is 1 second. At the start there are 1000 bacteria. How many will there be 10 minutes later? How many are there 2 hours later? The program EXPONENTIAL BACTERIA solves these problems. You INPUT the time T in seconds and your computer calculates the answer.

```
10 REM                   **************************
20 REM                   *                         *
30 REM                   * EXPONENTIAL BACTERIA *
40 REM                   *                         *
50 REM                   **************************
60 REM
70 REM
100 REM %%%%%%%%%%%%%%%%%%%%% SETTING UP %%%%%%%%%%%%%%%%%%%%%%%%%%%%%%%
110 LET A=0.00009627
120 PRINT CHR$(147) : REM CLEAR SCREEN
130 PRINT " EXPONENTIAL BACTERIA"
140 PRINT
150 PRINT "AT THE START THERE ARE 1000 BACTERIA "
160 LET Y=1000 : REM INITIAL NUMBER
170 PRINT
180 PRINT "TYPE IN TIME INTERVAL"
190 PRINT "IN SECONDS ";
200 INPUT T
210 PRINT
220 FOR I=0 TO T                        See the Appendix for some general notes.
230 LET Y=Y+A*Y
240 NEXT I
250 PRINT "AFTER";T;"SECONDS"
260 PRINT "THERE ARE ";INT(Y)
300 REM %%%%%%%%%%%%%%%%%%%%% ANOTHER GO? %%%%%%%%%%%%%%%%%%%%%%%%%%%%%
310 PRINT
320 PRINT " ANOTHER GO? Y OR N"
330 GET G$ : REM LET G$=INKEY$
340 IF G$<>"Y" AND G$<>"N" THEN GOTO 330
350 IF G$="Y" THEN GOTO 160
```

```
EXPONENTIAL BACTERIA

AT THE START THERE ARE
   1000 BACTERIA

TYPE IN TIME INTERVAL
IN SECONDS ? 600

AFTER 600 SECONDS
THERE ARE   1059

 ANOTHER GO? Y OR N

TYPE IN TIME INTERVAL
IN SECONDS ? 7200

AFTER 7200 SECONDS
THERE ARE   2000

 ANOTHER GO? Y OR N
```

Notice that the size of the colony doubles in 2 hours (or 7200 seconds). In fact if the time taken for a colony to double in size is D seconds then the value of A in the differential equation Y' = A*Y is 0.69315/D (approximately).

The reason why we called our program on bacteria EXPONENTIAL BACTERIA is that our differential equation has a solution which is given by

Y = C*EXP(A*T)

where T denotes time and C is a constant which can be determined by observation. We will not give details of why this is a solution; if you know a bit of calculus you should be able to verify this. We shall be content with approximate solutions obtained via the Euler-Cauchy method.

Of course life is not quite so simple. If the differential equation Y' = A*Y really did describe the rate of change in the number of bacteria then these bacteria would quickly fill the whole world. This is illustrated with the graph at the top of the next page.

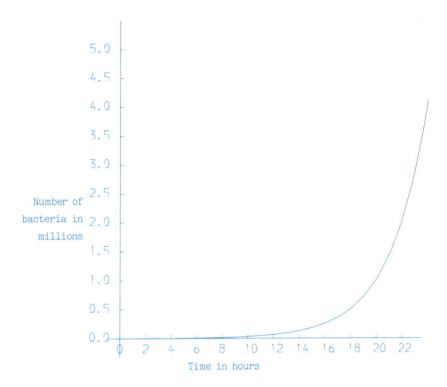

Migration, death, depletion of food, room and change of temperature all affect the number of bacteria. These factors should be incorporated into our differential equation to obtain more realistic results. We shall do this shortly.

Populations in general tend to grow "exponentially", just like bacteria. This is because the number of births is directly related to the size of the population. However, as with the bacteria, such exponential growth cannot continue unabated - the world and its enviroment is limited in size and resources.

A more accurate description of the rate of change of a population is given by the next differential equation.

    Y' = A*Y - B*Y*Y

In this model the number of births is again proportional to the size of the population (this is the A*Y term). On the other hand a certain fraction dies. This fraction varies according to the size of the population,

GETTING BIGGER ALL THE TIME

and in general it increases with the size of the population. We assume that this fraction is B*Y and so the number of deaths is (B*Y)*Y as given by the extra term the equation.

With this differential equation the population will not continue increasing for ever. The growth of the population is, in general, "S" shaped. Initially, when Y is relatively small, it grows exponentially. But as Y increases the effects of death cause the population to tend towards the value of A/B. Notice that if you put Y equal to A/B into the differential equation then you obtain Y' = 0. In other words the rate of change of the population is 0 and hence there is no change in the population size. Thus if the population size reaches the value A/B it remains at that value. Sometimes it never gets to this value but exceeds it, then goes below it, then exceeds it again, and so on. What happens depends on the values of A and B. Some graphs, for different values of A, are given below.

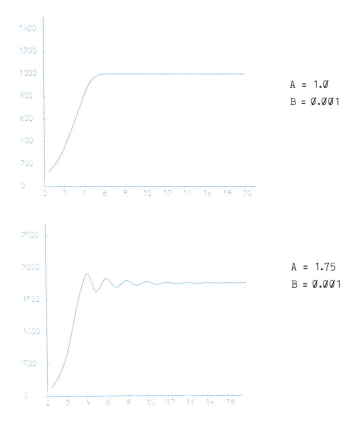

A = 1.0
B = 0.001

A = 1.75
B = 0.001

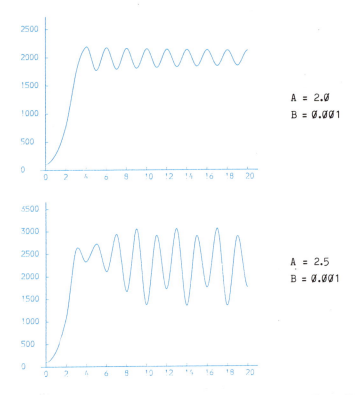

A = 2.0
B = 0.001

A = 2.5
B = 0.001

You can find out how a typical population grows or dies with the program GROWTH. This program uses the Euler-Cauchy method of solving the differential equation. You INPUT the values of A, B and the initial population size. The program then PRINTs out the population size over the next 24 periods. The main loop is based on the following equation.

$$Y_{NEW} = Y_{OLD} + A*Y_{OLD} - B*Y_{OLD}*Y_{OLD}$$

```
10 REM                     *********
20 REM                     *       *
30 REM                     * GROWTH *
40 REM                     *       *
50 REM                     *********
60 REM
70 REM
100 REM %%%%%%%%%%%%%%%%%%%%%% SETTING UP %%%%%%%%%%%%%%%%%%%%%%%%%%%%%%
110 PRINT CHR$(147); : REM CLEAR SCREEN
120 PRINT "      GROWTH"
130 PRINT
140 PRINT "  Y' = A*Y - B*Y*Y"
150 PRINT
```

```
160 PRINT "VALUE OF A";
170 INPUT A
180 PRINT
190 PRINT "VALUE OF B";
200 INPUT B
210 PRINT
220 PRINT "INITIAL POPULATION"
230 PRINT "SIZE ";
240 INPUT Y
250 PRINT
300 REM %%%%%%%%%%%%%%%%%%%%% CALCULATING %%%%%%%%%%%%%%%%%%%%%%%%%%%%%
310 FOR I=1 TO 24
320 LET Y=(1+A-B*Y)*Y
330 IF Y<0 THEN LET Y=0
340 PRINT INT(Y),
350 NEXT I
400 REM %%%%%%%%%%%%%%%%%%%%% ANOTHER GO? %%%%%%%%%%%%%%%%%%%%%%%%%%%%%
410 PRINT
420 PRINT " ANOTHER GO? Y OR N"
430 GET G$  : REM LET G$=INKEY$
440 IF G$<>"Y" AND G$<>"N" THEN GOTO 430
450 IF G$="Y" THEN GOTO 110
```

See the Appendix for some general notes.

```
           GROWTH

       Y' = A*Y - B*Y*Y

    VALUE OF A? 1.75

    VALUE OF B? .001

    INITIAL POPULATION
    SIZE ? 50

       135              353
       846             1610
      1834             1679
      1798             1711
      1777             1728
      1765             1738
      1758             1743
      1754             1746
      1752             1747
      1751             1748
      1750             1749
      1750             1749

       ANOTHER GO? Y OR N
```

You may prefer to plot a graph showing the size of the population as time changes. You can do this by incorporating the GRAPH PLOTTING program from the second chapter with the above GROWTH program.

Struggle for survival. When two or more species live together they often interact in their struggle for survival; for instance when one species eats another, as with foxes and rabbits. The rabbits live off the land and the foxes eat the rabbits. The differential equations that we could use to describe the change in population size of the rabbits and foxes are given below.

$R' = A*R - B*R*R - C*R*F$
$F' = -D*F + E*R*F$

Here R is the number of rabbits, F is the number of foxes while A, B, C, D and E are numbers depending on enviromental factors.

As an example we shall use the following equations.

$R' = 0.04*R - 0.00005*R*R - 0.002*R*F$
$F'. = -0.03*F + 0.0002*R*F$

If there were no foxes then the rabbit population would stabalise at about 800. Any foxes around ensure that there are fewer that 800 rabbits. If there were no rabbits then the foxes would soon die out; not immediately because foxes will eat berries and other plant foods when faced with starvation.

The program RABBITS AND FOXES shows you what happens to the number of rabbits and foxes month by month. You INPUT the number of rabbits and foxes at the start. You then have a choice. You may have the numbers printed out on your screen or you may have a visual display. In the visual display * is printed on your screen to indicate the number of rabbits and foxes. The horizontal position of * represents R/20, that is, one-twentieth of the number of rabbits. The vertical position indicates the value of F/2, that is, half the number of foxes. With the visual display you will see a spiral effect indicating that the number of rabbits and foxes increases and decreases repeatedly (see the diagram on the next page).

GETTING BIGGER ALL THE TIME

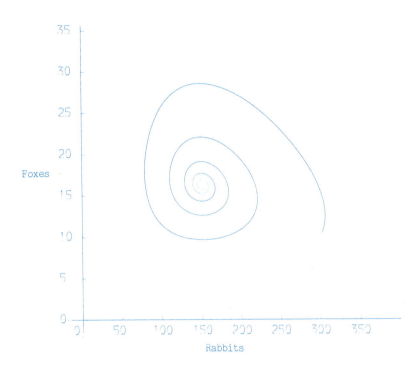

```
10 REM                    **********************
20 REM                    *                    *
30 REM                    * RABBITS AND FOXES  *
40 REM                    *                    *
50 REM                    **********************
60 REM
70 REM
100 REM %%%%%%%%%%%%%%%%%%%% SETTING UP %%%%%%%%%%%%%%%%%%%%%%%%%%%%
110 LET CS$=CHR$(147) : REM CODE FOR CLEAR SCREEN
120 LET PX=22 : REM NO. OF HORIZ PRINT POSITIONS
130 LET PY=23 : REM NO. OF VERT PRINT POSITIONS
140 LET A=0.04
150 LET B=0.00005
160 LET C=0.002
170 LET D=0.03
180 LET E=0.0002
190 PRINT CS$ : REM CLS
200 PRINT "   RABBITS AND FOXES"
210 PRINT
220 PRINT "HOW MANY RABBITS";
230 INPUT R
240 PRINT
250 PRINT "HOW MANY FOXES";
260 INPUT F
270 PRINT
280 PRINT
290 PRINT "OPTIONS:"
300 PRINT
```

Try putting B=0 and see what happens. Also, change the values of A, C, D and E.

INPUT the number of rabbits and foxes.

```
310 PRINT "1. NUMERICAL PRINTOUT"
320 PRINT
330 PRINT "2. TEMPORARY"
340 PRINT "GRAPHICAL DISPLAY"
350 PRINT
360 PRINT "3. PERMANENT"
370 PRINT "GRAPHICAL DISPLAY"
380 PRINT
390 PRINT "WHICH OPTION";
400 INPUT T
410 LET T=INT(T)
420 IF T<1 OR T>3 THEN GOTO 400
430 PRINT
440 IF T>1 THEN GOTO 610
500 REM %%%%%%%%%%%%%%%%%%%%%% OPTION 1 %%%%%%%%%%%%%%%%%%%%%%%%%%%%%%%%
510 PRINT "RABBITS    FOXES"
520 PRINT
530 FOR I=1 TO 20
540 PRINT INT(R);TAB(10) INT(F)
550 GOSUB 910
560 NEXT I
570 GOTO 840
600 REM %%%%%%%%%%%%%%%%%%%%%% OPTIONS 2&3 %%%%%%%%%%%%%%%%%%%%%%%%%%%%%
610 PRINT CS$; : REM CLS
620 POKE 36879,170 : REM SCREEN COLOUR
630 PRINT "  RABBITS AND FOXES"
640 FOR I=1 TO 500
650 LET V=INT(F/2)
660 IF V>PY-2 THEN LET V=PY-2
670 IF V<=0 THEN LET V=0
680 LET U=INT(R/20)
690 IF U>PX-1 THEN LET U=PX-1
700 IF U<=0 THEN LET U=0
710 GOSUB 1010 : REM PLOT U,V
720 GOSUB 910
730 IF T=2 THEN GOSUB 1110
740 NEXT I
800 REM %%%%%%%%%%%%%%%%%%%%%% ANOTHER GO? %%%%%%%%%%%%%%%%%%%%%%%%%%%%%
810 GET G$ : REM LET G$=INKEY$
820 IF G$="" THEN GOTO 810
830 PRINT CS$ : REM CLS
840 PRINT " ANOTHER GO? Y OR N";
850 GET G$ : REM LET G$=INKEY$
860 IF G$<>"Y" AND G$<>"N" THEN GOTO 850
870 IF G$="Y" THEN GOTO 190
880 END : REM STOP
900 REM %%%%%%%%%%%%%%%%%%%%%% CALCULATING %%%%%%%%%%%%%%%%%%%%%%%%%%%%%
910 LET R=(1+A-B*R-C*F)*R
920 LET F=(1-D+E*R)*F
930 RETURN
1000 REM %%%%%%%%%%%%%%%%%%%%% PLOT VIA POKE %%%%%%%%%%%%%%%%%%%%%%%%%%%
1010 POKE 8164+(PEEK(44)>=18)*3584+U-22*V,42
1020 RETURN
1100 REM %%%%%%%%%%%%%%%%%%%%% UNPLOT VIA POKE %%%%%%%%%%%%%%%%%%%%%%%%%
1110 POKE 8164+(PEEK(44)>=18)*3584+U-22*V,32
1120 RETURN
```

Three options are available.

This prints out the number of rabbits and foxes over a 20 month period.

This plots the number of rabbits and foxes over a 500 month period.

See the Appendix for further notes.

The display will remain until any key is pressed.

This is the Euler-Cauchy method of calculating the values of R and F.

If PLOTting via POKE, put in the appropriate values.

```
    RABBITS AND FOXES

HOW MANY RABBITS? 340

HOW MANY FOXES? 35


OPTIONS:

1. NUMERICAL PRINTOUT

2. TEMPORARY
GRAPHICAL DISPLAY

3. PERMANENT
GRAPHICAL DISPLAY

WHICH OPTION? 1
```

```
    RABBITS      FOXES
     340          35
     324          36
     308          37
     292          38
     277          39
     263          40
     248          41
     235          41
     222          42
     209          42
     198          43
     186          43
     176          43
     166          44
     156          44
     148          44
     139          43
     132          43
     125          43
     118          43
```

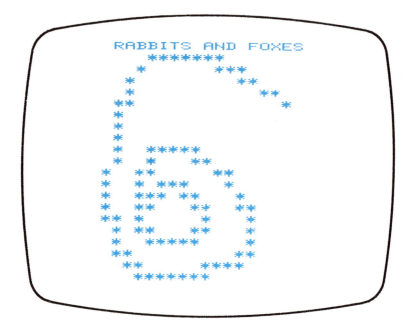

Virus. Using some of the ideas concerning rabbits and foxes we can create an interesting game. A game that is not intended to be fully representative of real life.

In the game VIRUS, a new virus (possibly extraterrestrial) is sweeping the country and you have a room full of infected patients. This virus produces rogue cells. These rogue cells reproduce and affect the healthy cells converting them into rogue cells. A seriously infected patient develops symptoms which are too horrific to describe. With a low blood count the patient soon dies.

A new drug has been found, but there is no time to go through all the usual tests for new drugs. It is a cytotoxic drug. Thus, not only does it destroy rogue cells, it also destroys healthy cells. Experiments so far have shown that more than 600 milligrams of the drug will kill the patient. In addition, the drug remains in the body for some time. In fact, after an hour only about 83% of the drug in a patient is used up.

Your patient's blood count has already dropped down to about 7000. If it falls below 1500 the patient will die. To help you, your computer gives an hourly report giving you a blood count and the number of rogue cells. Each hour, you may give your patient some of the new drug. But remember, more than 600 milligrams will kill the patient. Also, remember the cumulative effect of the drug.

Occasionally a patient has an anaphylactic reaction to the drug and dies immediately.

Your goal is to save as many patients as possible.

The program VIRUS is based on the following two differential equations.

$X' = 0.01*X - 0.000001*X*X - 0.0001*X*Y - 0.0005*X*D$
$Y' = -0.005*Y - 0.0000001*Y*Y + 0.00001*X*Y - 0.001*Y*D$

Here X denotes the number of healthy cells, Y the number of rogue cells and D the quantity of drug in the body. These differential equations are based on a 12 minute interval. They are therefore used 5 times to obtain an hourly report. During each 12 minute interval the value of D is decreased by multiplying it by 0.7. This means that after an hour there is still about 17% of the drug affecting the cells.

```
10 REM                      ********
20 REM                      *      *
30 REM                      * VIRUS *
40 REM                      *      *
50 REM                      ********
60 REM
70 REM
100 REM %%%%%%%%%%%%%%%%%%%%%% SETTING UP %%%%%%%%%%%%%%%%%%%%%%%%%%%%%%
110 LET C$=CHR$(147) : REM CODE FOR CLEAR SCREEN
120 LET B$=CHR$(31)  : REM BLUE
130 LET R$=CHR$(28)  : REM RED
140 LET M$=CHR$(156) : REM MAGENTA
150 LET G$=CHR$(30)  : REM GREEN
160 LET C$=CHR$(159) : REM CYAN
170 LET Y$=CHR$(158) : REM YELLOW
```

If colours are available on your computer then put in the appropriate code numbers; otherwise delete B$, R$, etc.

```
180 PRINT CS$ : REM CLS
190 PRINT R$+"        VIRUS"
200 PRINT
210 PRINT B$+"YOU HAVE 10 PATIENTS"
220 PRINT
230 PRINT B$+" DRUGS, UP TO 600 MG"
240 PRINT B$+" MAY HELP"
250 PRINT
260 PRINT R$+"WITH A BLOOD COUNT OF"
270 PRINT R$+"LESS THAN 1500 THE"
280 PRINT R$+"PATIENT DIES"
```

This gives a brief outline of the rules.

```
290 PRINT
300 PRINT G$+" SAVE AS MANY AS YOU"
310 PRINT G$+" CAN   -   GOOD LUCK"
320 PRINT
330 PRINT Y$+"  PRESS Y TO START"
340 GET H$ : REM LET H$=INKEY$
350 IF H$<>"Y" THEN GOTO 340
360 LET PATIENT=0
370 LET T=9.1 : REM HOUR TIME
380 LET T$="A.M."
390 LET N=0 : REM SAVED PATIENTS
400 REM %%%%%%%%%%%%%%%%%%%%% START %%%%%%%%%%%%%%%%%%%%%%%%%%%%%%%
410 PRINT CS$ : REM CLS
420 LET PATIENT=PATIENT+1
430 PRINT B$+"VIRUS PATIENT ";PATIENT
440 PRINT
450 LET X=6900+INT(RND(1)*200) : REM BLOOD COUNT
460 LET Y=100+INT(RND(1)*20) : REM ROGUE CELLS
470 LET D=0 : REM DRUGS
480 LET P=RND(1)
500 REM %%%%%%%%%%%%%%%%%%%%% DISPLAY %%%%%%%%%%%%%%%%%%%%%%%%%%%%
510 PRINT R$+"BLOOD COUNT";X
520 PRINT
530 PRINT M$+"ROGUE CELLS";Y
540 PRINT
550 PRINT C$+"  *  *  *  *  *  *  *"
560 PRINT
600 REM %%%%%%%%%%%%%%%%%%%%% CHECK FOR ENDING %%%%%%%%%%%%%%%%%%%
610 IF X<1500 THEN GOTO 1210
620 IF Y=0 THEN GOTO 1310
700 REM %%%%%%%%%%%%%%%%%%%%% CALCULATING %%%%%%%%%%%%%%%%%%%%%%%%
710 PRINT B$+"TIME: ";INT(T+1-12*INT(T/12));T$
720 PRINT
730 PRINT G$+"QUANTITY OF DRUG?"
740 INPUT Q
750 PRINT
760 LET D=D+Q
770 IF D>0 AND P<0.08 THEN GOTO 1010
780 IF D>600 THEN GOTO 1110
790 FOR I=1 TO 5
800 LET X=X*(1.01-0.0001*(0.01*X+Y+5*D))
810 LET Y=Y*(0.995-0.001*(0.01*(0.01*Y-X)+D))
820 LET D=0.7*D
830 NEXT I
840 IF Y<0 THEN LET Y=0
850 LET X=INT(X)
860 LET Y=INT(Y+0.3)
870 LET T=T+1
880 LET T$="P.M."
890 IF 2*INT(T/24)=INT(T/12) THEN LET T$="A.M."
900 LET T1=INT(T-24*INT(T/24))
910 IF T1=23 THEN LET T$="MIDNIGHT"
920 IF T1=11 THEN LET T$="MIDDAY"
930 GOTO 510
```

There is an 8% chance that a patient has an anaphylactic reaction to the drug. Change this if you like in line 770.

```
1000 REM %%%%%%%%%%%%%%%%%%%%% ANAPHYLACTIC REACTION %%%%%%%%%%%%%%%%%%%%
1010 PRINT R$+"YOUR PATIENT HAD AN"
1020 PRINT R$+"ANAPHYLACTIC REACTION"
1030 PRINT
1040 GOTO 1210
1100 REM %%%%%%%%%%%%%%%%%%%%% PATIENT OVERDRUGGED %%%%%%%%%%%%%%%%%%%%
1110 PRINT R$+"YOUR PATIENT HAS BEEN"
1120 PRINT R$+"     OVERDRUGGED"
1130 PRINT
1200 REM %%%%%%%%%%%%%%%%%%%%% PATIENT PASSED AWAY %%%%%%%%%%%%%%%%%%%%
1210 PRINT R$+"YOUR PATIENT HAS JUST"
1220 PRINT R$+"     PASSED AWAY"
1230 PRINT
1240 GOTO 1410
1300 REM %%%%%%%%%%%%%%%%%%%%% PATIENT SAVED %%%%%%%%%%%%%%%%%%%%%%%%%%
1310 PRINT G$+"     WELL  DONE"
1320 PRINT
1330 PRINT G$+"YOUR PATIENT IS WELL"
1340 PRINT
1350 LET N=N+1
1400 REM %%%%%%%%%%%%%%%%%%%%% NEXT PATIENT %%%%%%%%%%%%%%%%%%%%%%%%%%%
1410 PRINT Y$+" *  *  *  *  *  *  *"
1420 PRINT
1430 IF PATIENT>9 THEN GOTO 1510
1440 PRINT C$+"          PRESS Y"
1450 PRINT C$+"FOR YOUR NEXT PATIENT"
1460 GET H$ : REM LET H$=INKEY$
1470 IF H$<>"Y" THEN GOTO 1460
1480 GOTO 410
1500 REM %%%%%%%%%%%%%%%%%%%%% ANOTHER GO? %%%%%%%%%%%%%%%%%%%%%%%%%%%%
1510 PRINT B$+"  OUT OF 10 PATIENTS"
1520 PRINT B$+"   YOU SAVED";N
1530 PRINT B$+"   IN ";INT(T-9);"HOURS"
1540 PRINT
1550 PRINT C$+" ANOTHER GO?  Y OR N"+B$
1560 GET H$ : REM LET H$=INKEY$
1570 IF H$<>"Y" AND H$<>"N" THEN GOTO 1560
1580 IF H$="Y" THEN GOTO 180
```

The program VIRUS contains no sound effects; add these, if available, wherever you like.

```
         VIRUS

  YOU HAVE 10 PATIENTS

   DRUGS, UP TO 600 MG
   MAY HELP

  WITH A BLOOD COUNT OF
  LESS THAN 1500 THE
  PATIENT DIES

   SAVE AS MANY AS YOU
   CAN    -    GOOD LUCK

    PRESS Y TO START
```

```
  VIRUS PATIENT   1

  BLOOD COUNT 7025

  ROGUE CELLS 118

   *  *  *  *  *  *  *

  TIME:   10 A.M.

  QUANTITY OF DRUG?
  ? 600

  BLOOD COUNT 2761

  ROGUE CELLS 17

    *  *  *  *  *  *  *
```

```
* * * * * * *
TIME:   11 P.M.
QUANTITY OF DRUG?
?80
BLOOD COUNT 1179
ROGUE CELLS 2
* * * * * * *
YOUR PATIENT HAS JUST
      PASSED AWAY
* * * * * * *
         PRESS Y
FOR YOUR NEXT PATIENT
```

```
* * * * * * *
TIME:   5 P.M.
QUANTITY OF DRUG?
? 200
BLOOD COUNT 1607
ROGUE CELLS 0
* * * * * * *
      WELL   DONE
YOUR PATIENT IS WELL
* * * * * * *
         PRESS Y
FOR YOUR NEXT PATIENT
```

```
*   *   *   *   *   *   *

TIME:   4 P.M.

QUANTITY OF DRUG?
? 200

BLOOD COUNT 1665

ROGUE CELLS 0

*   *   *   *   *   *   *

      WELL  DONE

YOUR PATIENT IS WELL

*   *   *   *   *   *   *

   OUT OF 10 PATIENTS
   YOU SAVED 9
   IN   391 HOURS

ANOTHER GO?  Y OR N
```

APPENDIX – CONVERTING YOUR PROGRAM

notes to help you convert the programs

The purpose of this appendix is to help you make any necessary alterations to the programs in this book. Each program has been written so that it is readily adaptable for your home computer.

Practicalities. Type out the program, looking at the REMarks, and make any obvious necessary changes as you go along. You will find information in the rest of this appendix for any changes that may need to be made. Be careful when typing the program; be particularly careful with colons and semicolons, with the number "1" and letter "I" and finally with the number "Ø" and letter "O".

After you have typed out the program it is wise to SAVE it - just in case. After that, try RUNning it. If there are any errors, first check that you have typed out the program correctly. Then check that any necessary alterations have been made. The programs have been fully tested and should RUN.

Finally, polish the program off by taking full advantage of any sound or colour available on your home computer.

REMarks. Many REMarks have been included in the programs. These may be safely omitted if desired. In some cases (for example for some Sinclair microcomputers) you will need to delete the REMarks following a statement. Some of the REMarks provide an alternative form of BASIC.

PRINT CS$ This is often used. Its purpose is to clear the screen and move the cursor to the home position (the upper-left corner of the screen).

On many home computers CLS is available, on others you will need to use the appropriate code. For example, for the Commodore computers we LET CS$=CHR$(147), although an alternative is available. For a few machines the correct code is CHR$(12). This applies, for example, to the BBC microcomputer, the Nascom II and the UK 101, although the first two also have CLS as an alternative. CHR$(12) clears the screen on the Research Machines' computers but moves the cursor to the lower-left corner of the screen. The newer versions use CHR$(31) to clear the screen and move the cursor to the upper-left corner.

For some microcomputers the screen is cleared by using the ESCape character, CHR$(27), followed by another character. Thus, for example, for the Apple we have CS$=CHR$(27)+CHR$(64), although HOME also clears the screen. For the Sirius 1 and Victor 9000 use CS$=CHR$(27)+CHR$(69).

Check your manual to find out what you should use to clear the screen.

PRINT HM$ This is used to move the cursor to its home position (upper-left corner of the screen) without clearing the screen.

If available you can use PRINT AT 0,0. This applies, for example, to the Sinclair microcomputers. Otherwise you will need to know the appropriate CHR$ code. For example, the appropriate code for the Commodore computers is CHR$(19), although an alternative is available. For the Atom the code is $30, while for the TRS 80 the code is CHR$(28). For the newer Research Machines' computers use CHR$(29). For the Apple the home position is obtained by using VTAB 1:HTAB 1.

For some microcomputers the home position is achieved by using the ESCape character, CHR$(27), followed by another character. This applies, for example, to the Sirius 1 and Victor 9000 where we would use HM$=CHR$(27)+CHR$(72).

Reverse or inverse video. Occasionally the reverse or inverse of a character is used in the screen display. While this is not strictly necessary it does enhance some programs.

On many home computers there is a code which turns the reverse or inverse video on. For example, Commodore computers use CHR$(18) to turn it on, and CHR$(146) to turn it off. Some computers use the ESCape character, CHR$(27), followed by another character. The Apple uses the words INVERSE and NORMAL to turn the inverse video on and off. For Sinclair's ZX 81 the inverse characters are obtained by adding 128 to the CODE of the character. Thus CHR$(38) is an A, while CHR$(166) is an inverse A. For the Spectrum you can use CHR$(20) + CHR$(1) to turn the inverse video on and CHR$(20) + CHR$(0) to turn it off.

APPENDIX - CONVERTING YOUR PROGRAM

GET G$: REM LET G$=INKEY$ This is used to get a one-character string without the need to press RETURN, NEWLINE or ENTER. If no character is pending at the keyboard then a null string is returned.

For example, the following may appear in a program.

```
510 GET G$ : REM LET G$=INKEY$
520 IF G$="Z" THEN LET TH=TH-1
530 IF G$="C" THEN LET TH=TH+1
540 IF G$="B" THEN LET A=A-1
550 IF G$="M" THEN LET A=A+1
```

On line 510, we do not want the program to wait until a key is pressed. In other words we want the program to go on to the next line if no key is pressed.

On some home computers this is achieved by one of the following.

```
GET G$            (not on the Apple)
LET G$=INKEY$
LET G$=GET$(0)
LET G$=INKEY$(0)
LET G$=INPUT$(1)
```

On some microcomputers you may need to declare G$="" beforehand; check with your manual.

If one of the above is not available, or if it does not give the desired result then you will need to use PEEK or USR. For example, with the Apple PEEK(-16384)-128 gives the ASCII code of the key pressed. Thus we could use the following

```
LET G$=CHR$(PEEK(-16384)-128)
```

This should be followed, after G$ is used, by POKE -16368,0 to clear the buffer.

Check your manual to find out what to use.

Occasionally you will see the following two lines in a program.

```
540 GET G$ : REM LET G$=INKEY$
550 IF G$<>"Y" AND G$<>"N" THEN GOTO 540
```

In such a situation we <u>do</u> want the program to wait until a key is pressed.

On some computers these two lines may, if desired, be incorporated into one line. For example, in the Tandy TRS 80 we could simply use

    540 G$=INSTR$(1)

The GET G$ in the Apple waits until a key is pressed and so the two lines above could be replaced with the following single one.

    540 GET G$

Check you manual to find out what is available.

INPUT The INPUT statement allows the computer to get data from the person RUNning the program. The program will stop, usually print a question mark on the screen, and wait for the person to type in the data and press RETURN, NEWLINE or ENTER. The response usually appears on the screen. Sometimes (as with the Sinclair microcomputers) the response does not remain on the screen after NEWLINE or ENTER has been pressed. If this is the case then simply add an extra line after each INPUT statement to PRINT out the INPUT. For example, suppose we had the following lines in our program.

    150 PRINT "TYPE IN NUMBER";
    160 INPUT X
    170 IF X>0 THEN GOTO 600

If the value of X does not remain on the screen then simply add the following extra line.

    165 PRINT X

On many home computers you can use a prompt in the INPUT statement. Thus in the example above we could replace lines 150 and 160 by the following line.

    150 INPUT "TYPE IN NUMBER";X

In this way you can often shorten some of the programs.

RND(1) We have used RND(1) to denote a random number between 0 and 1. Some microcomputers simply use RND, if this is so then you will need to make the appropriate changes.

To obtain a random number in the range A to B we have used the expession

    A + (B-A)*RND(1)

APPENDIX – CONVERTING YOUR PROGRAM

Some computers allow you to use the following instead.

    A + RND(B-A)

Some computers produce a fixed sequence of random numbers if you use RND(1). In such a case you will need to replace RND(1) by RND(X) where X is some randomly chosen integer.

Check your manual to find out what you should do to obtain random numbers.

DIM Arrays have always been dimensioned in the programs. On many microcomputers this is not necessary if the dimension is 10 or less. In addition, we have used one line for each array to be dimensioned. Often you can place all the DIMension statements on one line. If both of these facilities are available then, for example, the following lines

    110 DIM A(7)
    130 DIM B$(20)
    140 DIM C(15)

may be replaced by the following line.

    110 DIM A(7),B$(20),C(15)

Check with your manual as to what you are allowed to do.

PLOT U,V For computers with PLOT facilities we have assumed that the origin is at the bottom-left corner of the screen. If your computer has its origin at the upper-left corner then the picture may appear upside down unless you make some changes. For example, by using PLOT U,SY-V instead of PLOT U,V.

String concatenation. The plus sign has been used for string concatenation. Some microcomputers use a comma or an ampersand. Check your manual to find out what you should use and make the appropriate changes if necessary.

Substrings of strings. The use of this has been avoided. It is certainly non-standard amongst the various BASICs around.

Spaces 1. In Microsoft BASIC printed numbers are always followed by a space. Positive numbers are preceded by a space. Negative numbers are preceded by a minus sign. Some BASICs (for example Sinclair BASIC) are not like this.

APPENDIX – CONVERTING YOUR PROGRAM

The programs in this book have <u>usually</u> assumed that the numbers will be printed as in Microsoft BASIC. If your machine's BASIC is different then you may need to add spaces after and/or before a number is printed. For example, the following might be a typical line.

    140 PRINT "THE VALUE IS";V

You may need to change this to the following, to obtain a readable display.

    140 PRINT "THE VALUE IS ";V

Sometimes the space following a number in Microsoft BASIC is a nuisance. To prevent this space being printed we have often converted a number into a STRing and then printed the string. For example,

    420 PRINT STR$(X);

Sometimes it is safe to replace such a line by the following line.

    420 PRINT X;

Find out yourself by experimenting.

Spaces 2. Many BASICs allow you to have no spaces in a line. For example, instead of the following line

    750 IF G$="Y" THEN GOTO 180

you could have

    750 IFG$="Y"THENGOTO180

Doing this will certainly save space if that is crucial to you.

LET On most computers LET is optional (it is not on the Sinclair microcomputers). We have used LET throughout the programs. If LET is optional then you may omit it, if you like. For example, the following two lines

    690 LET A=0
    700 IF B<0 THEN LET A=1

may be replaced by these two lines.

    690 A=0
    700 IF B<0 THEN A=1

APPENDIX - CONVERTING YOUR PROGRAM

IF .. THEN GOTO The GOTO following an IF THEN statement is not necessary on most home computers. You may omit it if you wish. For example, the line

    310 IF G$="" THEN GOTO 300

may be replaced by the following line.

    310 IF G$="" THEN 300

On some computers you may instead delete THEN and leave GOTO (on a few computers this is obligatory). Thus, for example, the original line above may (and in some cases should) be replaced by the following line.

    310 IF G$="" GOTO 300

Experiment and check your manual to see what you may or should do.

Multiple statements. Most home computers allow you to have several statements on one line. These statements are usually separated by a colon. All the programs in this book have been written without multiple statements on a line. The exception being that REMarks have sometimes been included as a second statement. These REMarks can be safely omitted from the programs. Many of the programs can be shortened, possibly improved, by using multiple statements on a line. For example, the following lines

    720 LET A=0
    730 LET B=0.002
    740 LET X=0.1
    750 IF Y<0 THEN LET Z=0
    760 IF Y<0 THEN GOTO 910

may be condensed to the following two lines.

    720 LET A=0:LET B=0.002:LET X=0.1
    750 IF Y<0 THEN LET Z=0:GOTO 910

IF .. THEN .. ELSE This has not been used in any of the programs. If it is available on your home computer then you could use it to shorten one or two programs. As an example, the folowing two lines

    680 IF K<0 THEN GOTO 210
    690 GOTO 310

could be replaced by the following single line.

    680 IF K<0 THEN GOTO 210 ELSE GOTO 310

APPENDIX - CONVERTING YOUR PROGRAM

Brackets or parentheses. Brackets have always been included in all functions. On the Sinclair machines brackets are not necessary for.functions such as TAB, VAL, SIN. You may, if you wish, omit brackets on such machines; but take care - ocassionally the brackets are necessary.

NEXT I On some computers you do not need to specify a variable after a NEXT, as in NEXT I. By <u>not</u> specifying the variable the program will run faster, sometimes considerably faster.

Shortening the programs. The programs in this book have been written so that they are readily adaptable to your home computer. Consequently they are not as "neat" or "short" as they would be if they had been written for one specific machine.

Many of the suggestions given earlier on in this chapter will apply to your computer. Using them you can shorten, and possibly improve, many of the programs in this book. You will find that you can probably shorten each program by one-quarter or perhaps even by one-half of its length.

Part of the fun of computing is rewriting programs and adding your own personal touch.

Some extra notes for the VIC 20. A few of the programs use high resolution graphics. For these you will need to add 3K or more of memory.

WARNING. If you add 8K or more memory then the high resolution area is where the machine wants to store its BASIC. You must therefore move the BASIC area by using pointer 44. So, before typing or LOADing one of these programs, type the following.

POKE 44,32:POKE 8192,0:NEW

Check that you have typed it correctly and then press RETURN. If you have already typed a program without following the above instructions then SAVE it, follow the above instructions, and then LOAD it.

Finally, if for some reason one of the high resolution programs stops while in the middle of RUNning, you will just see nonsense. The remedy is to press the RUN STOP and the RESTORE keys simultaneously.

WHERE IT IS

an index

air resistance, 153
alternating series, 18
anaphylactic reaction, 179
APPROXIMATE GAME ANALYSIS, 82
Archimedes, 18
arithmetic sequence, 7
ARITHMETIC SEQUENCES, 8
arithmetic series, 8

bacteria, 167
BANK QUEUES, 116
beer drinking game, 85
BOUNCING BALL, 149
BOUTIQUEUES, 123

CALCULATING SIN(X), 20
card matching, 66
cartesian coordinates, 30
caterpillar on elastic, 17
Cauchy, A.L., 148
CLS, 185
combination of permutations, 88
common difference, 7
common ratio, 10
commutative group, 91
contour maps, 138
CONTOURS, 140
convergent series, 16
coordinates, 30

cumulative distribution function, 111
customer arrival rate, 108
CUSTOMER ARRIVALS I, 108
CUSTOMER ARRIVALS II, 110
CUSTOMER ARRIVALS III, 113
customer service rate, 115
cycles, 100
cytotoxic drug, 178

delta-epsilon approach, 148
Descartes, R., 30
determinant, 60
differential equation, 145
DIM, 189
distribution function, 111
divergent series, 16
domination, 74

equilateral triangle, 12
Euler, L., 19, 148
Euler-Cauchy method, 148
EXPONENTIAL BACTERIA, 168
exponential distribution, 115
exponential function, 16
exponential increase, 16
exponential series, 23

fair game, 68
FALLING STONE, 147

FLIGHT, 154
FOUR SQUARES, 92
foxes, 174
function, 29
function of two variables, 129

games of strategy, 65
game theory, 65
geometric progression, 10
geometric sequence, 10
GEOMETRIC SEQUENCES, 11
geometric series, 10
GET G$, 187
GOTO, 191
GRAPH PLOTTING, 33
graphs, 30
groups, 87
GROWTH, 172

harmonic series, 14
HARMONIC SERIES, 15
how to make money!, 74
hypotenuse, 52

identity
  matrix, 60
  permutation, 89
INKEY$, 187
INPUT, 188
INPUT$, 187
INSTR$, 188
INTELLIGENCE TEST, 24
intelligence tests, 24
inter-arrival time, 107
inverse of a permutation, 90
inverse video, 186
INVESTMENT GAME, 76

Leibnitz, G.W., 18
LET, 190

linear programming, 70
lines, 107
loving husband?, 18

matching pennies, 66
matrices, 60
matrix, 60
  determinant of, 60
  identity, 60
  payoff, 66
MATRIX INVESTIGATION, 61
minimax point, 68
modified Euler-Cauchy method, 148
monkey saddle, 134
Monte-Carlo process, 107

optimal strategy, 69
ORBIT, 161
order of a permutation, 89

payoff matrix, 66
permutations, 87
  combination of, 88
  commutative, 91
  group of, 90
  identity, 89
  inverse of, 90
  order of, 89
PI, 18
polar bees, 39
polar coordinates, 39
polar function, 40
polar graph, 40
POLAR GRAPHICS, 43
PLOT, 189
plotting a graph, 30
Poisson arrival, 112
Poisson, S.D., 112
PRINT CS$, 185
PRINT HM$, 186

WHERE IT IS

probability distribution
  function, 111
Pythagoras' theorem, 52

QUEUE ANALYSIS, 121
queues, 107

RABBITS AND FOXES, 175
radian, 19
rate of change, 145
rate of growth, 167
relief maps, 138
REMarks, 185
reverse video, 186
right-angled triangle, 52
RND, 188
RND(1), 188

sequence
  arithmetic, 7
  geometric, 11
SEQUENCES AND SERIES, 22
series, 8
  alternating, 18
  arctangent, 23
  arithmetic, 8
  convergent, 16
  cosine, 23
  divergent, 16
  exponential, 23
  geometric, 10
  harmonic, 14
  natural logarithm, 23
  PI, 18
  sine, 20
Sharp, 19

silver dollars game, 66
simplex method, 70
simulation, 107
SINCLAIR GRAPH PLOTTING, 36
SINCLAIR POLAR GRAPHICS, 46
sine, 19
SIN(X) series, 20
SIXTEEN SQUARES PUZZLE, 97
snowflakes, 12
solution of differential
  equation, 146
spaces, 189
strategy, 70
strictly determined games, 68
string concatenation, 189
struggle for survival, 174
substrings, 189
SURFACES, 135

terms, 7
transpositions, 96
TREASURE HUNT, 54
treasure island, 51
TWENTY-FIVE SQUARES PUZZLE, 103
two-finger morra, 66
two-person zero-sum game, 66
TWO-PERSON ZERO-SUM GAMES, 70

value of game, 68
VIC 20 GRAPH PLOTTING, 37
VIC 20 warning, 192
virus, 178
VIRUS, 179

warning for VIC 20, 192

ZX 81 INVESTMENT GAME, 79